Sex, Lies
& Statistics

BROOKE MAGNANTI

More books by this author

As Belle de Jour

Secret Diary of a London Call Girl

Further Adventures of a London Call Girl

Playing the Game

Belle de Jour's Guide to Men

Belle's Best Bits

As Brooke Magnanti

The Turning Tide

You Don't Know Me

To everyone who tried to keep this book from being published.

You failed.

CONTENTS

Foreword   vii

Glossary   ix

Introduction   1

Chapter 1   5

Chapter 2   17

Chapter 3   34

Chapter 4   49

Chapter 5   62

Chapter 6   76

Chapter 7   90

Afterword   123

Acknowledgments   133

About the Author   134

Citations   135

FOREWORD TO THE US EDITION

by Maggie McNeill

Mark Twain's witticism about statistics being the worst kind of lies is too familiar to need repeating. But while in his time it may have been a bit of an exaggeration for humorous effect, in ours it has become a plain fact. Ideologues who wish to lie convincingly have learned that fake "statistics" are very good at persuading the mathematically-illiterate to embrace ideas they're already predisposed to believe.

That goes double when the subject is sex and quadruple when the subject is sex work; it seems that no figure, no matter how outlandish nor how blatantly in defiance of the laws of logic, psychology and physiology, is unbelievable to the average person as long as it serves to advance the narrative that sex is dirty and harmful, and that anyone involved in the sex industry must be either a victim or a villain.

If the subject were anything else, journalists (and perhaps even some politicians) faced with extreme claims involving many millions of people would almost certainly seek input from actual experts in the field. But due to the powerful and entrenched cultural stigmas surrounding sex, very few with the power to influence public opinion ever bother to consult sex workers about our own profession.

While there are many ethical academics who have produced sound research on sex work and sex in general, there are also many unethical ones who don't hesitate to craft bogus "studies" designed to produce false results intended to uphold an anti-sex agenda; how is a person with experience in neither science nor the sex industry to tell the difference?

That's why social media have been such important tools in the advancement of sex workers' rights; they have allowed sex workers to speak for ourselves despite the opposition of those with a vested interest in maintaining the status quo. Blogs and Twitter in particular have provided sex workers with a platform from which we can speak directly to the public, sharing our experiences and debunking the damned lies used by prohibitionists to raise and maintain public support for the criminalization of our work, lives and associates.

Unfortunately, the members of anti-sex crowd aren't stupid; they can use social media as well, and they're backed by authoritarian individuals, organizations and governments with very deep pockets. In the past 20 years an entire industry has grown up around convincing the voters that the sex workers who speak so eloquently about the harms done by criminalization are either lying, mentally ill, a tiny and unrepresentative minority, or all three. And one of their chief means of accomplishing this is the generation and dissemination of false "facts" and unsupported "theories."

In the face of this assault, sex workers and ethical academics are faced with the daunting double task of not only getting the truth out, but also of debunking the myths and bogus statistics with which the prohibitionists hope to confuse and bamboozle those who don't have inside knowledge that comes from either deep study or lived experience.

That is why this book is so incredibly important. Dr. Brooke Magnanti is not only a former sex worker and an experienced activist with a broad, deep knowledge of the subject matter; she is also a trained scientist who can explain exactly how the anti-sex industry plays fast-and-loose with figures to make their lurid fantasies about sex, porn and sex work seem like sober facts in the eyes of those who don't know any better.

Dr. Magnanti has one more important credential: she's an engaging writer whose award-winning blog on her time as the London call girl Belle de Jour inspired several books and a hit television series, Secret Diary of a Call Girl. So even if math isn't your strong point, fear not; this book is written with the same style and wit that have made her a popular writer for over a decade, and strips away the dangerous nonsense the modern-day Puritans have used to cloak their moralistic crusade in the veneer of science.

GLOSSARY

Sex work
Any job where sexual labour is the product or service. Here, I use sex work to refer mainly to full-service providers (prostitution) but porn, exotic dance and many other jobs are also kinds of sex work.

Sex worker
Someone who directly engages in sex work, whose erotic capital is the product or service. Porn directors and escort managers may be employed in the sex industry, but they are not sex workers per se.

Decriminalization/Decrim
The elimination of all legal impediments to sex work. As seen in eg. New Zealand and New South Wales Australia, where sex workers may choose to work in (regulated) premises for others or in private premises for themselves. The preferred model endorsed by sex worker-led organizations, Amnesty International, the WHO, UNAids, and many others because it aids labor rights and sex worker safety.

Legalization
A system where sex work is only permitted by regulated workers in licensed premises, such as Nevada's brothels or Amsterdam's Red Light District. Not preferred by sex worker-led organizations due to a "two tier" effect criminalizing some workers and not others.

Swedish model (or Nordic model), partial criminalization
A model where customers of sex workers are explicitly criminalized, as seen in Sweden, Norway, France and Northern Ireland. Not preferred by sex worker-led organizations due to indirect criminalization of sex workers, and increased danger and stigmatization.

Full criminalization
In most of the US and a number of other countries, both the buying and selling of sex are illegal, and stigmatizing sex workers is common.

INTRODUCTION

Men, it has been well said, think in herds; it will be seen that they go mad in herds, while they only recover their senses slowly, and one by one.

Charles Mackay, "Extraordinary Popular Delusions and the Madness of Crowds"

When ancient cultures looked at the night sky they saw groups of stars, the way we do today. They drew imaginary lines between the stars to make pictures and tell stories. These pictures are known as constellations.

The stories behind constellations came with moral or cautionary undertones. One was the legend of the warrior Orion, placed among the heavens after his heroic death. Another was Cassiopeia, a vain queen suspended upside down in punishment for her self-obsession.

The pictures and the stories varied, depending on who was doing the looking. One of the most easily recognisable constellations is called the Big Dipper ... at least, it's called that if you grew up in the US. In the UK they know it as the Plough. Ancient Greeks saw the constellation as the tail of a bear and called it Ursa Major. The same collection of stars is a cart to Scandinavians, a coffin in Arabia, and a group of sages according to Hindu astronomy.

From our perspective on Earth, the stars of that constellation seem inextricably linked and for most of human history we had no way of knowing otherwise. The truth is the stars in the Big Dipper are not close together at all. It's the angle we view them from that makes them look related. In fact, they vary from between 78 to 124 light years away. They are also moving apart – in 50,000 years' time the Big Dipper won't look at all how it does now.

Constellations are what you make when you look at something from a particular angle at a particular time. Ancient people stared at the night sky for so long the dots seemed to make pictures, so we joined them up. The names the constellations have been given by different cultures reflect preoccupations of the people naming them. And while the stories may be entertaining or send a value message, they tell us nothing about the nature of the stars in themselves. They do not tell us the truth.

Humans as born storytellers make constellations from unrelated information all the time. But just because things seem to be connected to each other does not mean they are. It could be the angle, or the point in history, that creates the picture. We are hard-wired to see patterns and seek explanations. Sometimes this tendency leads to the wrong pictures being drawn.

When it comes to sex, the habit of making constellations is so pervasive that the truth can be hard to see. Myths, assumptions, and preconceptions dominate the discussion even when there is rational evidence to the contrary.

Sex is virtually a human universal. It's something most of us can claim, if not expertise, at least an enthusiastic amateur interest. But sex is a broad topic. Once out of the comfort zone of what we know first hand, all kinds of strange rumours can take hold. Once a rumour starts to spread it can be hard to stop. And before you know it, instead of correctly seeing balls of gas and flame in the night sky, we revert to mythology and fairy tales.

From the first rumours in the schoolyard, to the first fumblings in the dark, we learn about sex from the things we tell each other, and later from our own experiences.

As we get older and gain more insight, our gaze widens: from When will I have sex? What will it be like? How are other people doing it? to broader questions of sexual orientation, relationships, and more. We are as fascinated with the periphery of sex as with the nuts and bolts of it. Stories about prostitution, porn, and sex crimes are guaranteed to attract attention. Memoirs, exposés, and kiss-and-tells fly off the shelves. We get expertise however we can.

The less direct experience we have, the more we turn to gathering knowledge the old-fashioned way. The schoolyard way. 'I know someone who knows someone ...' once again becomes a believable source of information.

For example: it was once easy for people to believe second-hand stories and nasty rumours about gay people, because most straight people didn't know anyone who was out. As homosexuality became more accepted, the hatred began to wane. According to polls by the

Washington Post and ABC News, support for equal marriage rights has risen in direct proportion with the visibility of gay people. Sunshine is the best disinfectant, as they say.

Other groups, who are not yet as accepted, can still experience the full brunt of the rumour mill's attacks. Because a lot of people don't think they know any sex workers, stereotypes continue to hold sway. Who dares put their hand up to challenge what most people believe to be true? Where stigma is widespread, speaking up can be dangerous. Not everyone with direct knowledge is in a position to challenge the myths.

My own interest in this comes from two areas of my background: as a former sex worker, and as a scientist. I have been a call girl, and also an epidemiologist and forensic scientist. First-hand knowledge of the sex industry made me realize how much of what people believe about it is wrong. But it was being a scientist that made me realize *why*.

Why should it matter to you? Many reasons. The first is that a large proportion of women and gay men engage in types of sex work, either formally or casually, at some point during their lives. They are people we know and care about; they deserve to be safe.

In addition to this, the way society treats those on its margins says a lot about who we are. Sex workers are frequently already marginalized – people of color, trans people, migrants, drug users, disabled. Embracing dangerous "solutions" makes their lives more difficult than they need to be. Compassion and evidence should work together.

More generally, democracies depend on an informed public. People can't have first hand knowledge of everything, so turn to those they believe to be experts. The problem when it comes to emotive and controversial topics, especially sex, some of the people claiming to be experts are nothing of the kind.

As someone who devoted time to studying statistics, it is glaringly obvious when methods are being misused. I have seen up close and personal all the ways that bad information becomes news stories, political hot potatoes, and then hastily-passed laws – often with devastating real-world results.

Aristotle said truths have a natural tendency to prevail over their opposites, but with so much misinformation saturating the media, it takes effort. Fake news is halfway around the world before the truth gets its boots on. In situations where logic should rule, catchphrases, high emotions, and prejudice take control.

This book will examine the evidence behind topical stories we hear every day. In particular I will look at several tropes media seems to never get enough of: children and sexualization, porn and violence, sex work and trafficking. Research in these areas often overlaps, and I'll be investigating the good, the bad, and the ugly of the stats we hear thrown around all the time. Who's telling the truth, and who's trying to pass off fake numbers to sell their agenda? And whose agenda is it anyway?

The results, I think, may just surprise you.

CHAPTER 1

Did You Know...

- *Sexualization does not have a single definition, and is contextual*
- *Changes in modern media are not linked to earlier, or riskier, sex among teens*
- *Good research shows young people and parents are the best judges of what's appropriate*
- *Poor conclusions are being used to push ill-considered laws*

Let us begin with one of the most widespread myths. In almost every article touching on topics from social media to sex work, the arguments are underpinned with the belief that exposure to sexual images is invariably and irreversibly corrupting. The idea that the very sight of sex or sex workers turns women into mindless sexbots and men into drooling predators. This assumption is the foundation on which other myths are based.

Ridiculous, you might think. Nobody *really* believes that. But it totally permeates the discussion. There are articles implying this every week. Frequent books ignite panic about the sex college students are having on campus or that young single people in cities engage in. Younger ages, too, are thought to be at risk from sexual images and products, delivered through that portal of all things evil, the internet.

Consider Ariel Levy's *Living Dolls*, when she says of women who have 'their vaginas waxed ... their breasts enlarged' : 'I wish them many blissful and lubricious loops around the pole.' Sexualization then, however it's defined, is something these writers believe can't coexist with intelligence or informed decision-making.

There are many more such quasi-memoirs sprinkled with stats that turn out not to be true. Jessica Valenti's *Sex Object*, Caitlin Flanagan's *Girl Land*, Naomi Wolf's *Promiscuities*, Wendy Shalit's *Return to Modesty*. *American Hookup*. *The End of Sex*. And so on, in the same vein, one or two a year, every year.

Even the supposedly rational can fall for this myth. I experienced this personally, when an article in *BMJ Student* claimed that *Secret Diary of a Call Girl*, based on my memoirs, was causing students to go into sex work. The supposed "glamorizing" effects of a moderately popular show on ITV3 – a show that by the time of the article was already off the air - were suggested as a greater influence than the introduction of college tuition fees in the UK!

There were other problems with the paper, statistical ones: the number of sex working students in the UK was not directly surveyed, but extrapolated from a poll asking students at one university whether they knew anyone who had been a sex worker. See the problem? Not only could multiple people say they knew the same sex worker – thus inflating the total – no consideration was made for the fact that more sex workers are "out" than before, open about a job they might once have hidden.

Coverage of that article was widespread but logical analysis was completely absent. A closed news loop that fails to consider context is common with such stories. In part, because the people reporting on them do not have specific or relevant knowledge of the issues involved.

In fact the data around the sexualization trend are very shaky. When you look for outcomes most people fear the evidence just isn't there. In the few instances when reporters talk to young people, most of them have a more balanced approach than commentators give them credit for.

Sexualization is a difficult concept to define. To some, it could mean children imitating grown women, such as the furore over Beyoncé letting her daughter appear in a music video, or girls doing 'slut drops' on YouTube. To others, it could mean Playboy T-shirts and an avalanche of lurid pink. To others it's over-18s having casual sex or becoming sex workers.

Lack of a clear definition doesn't stop the judgments from coming though. The panic is far from new, in spite of what we're told about smartphones and Tinder. Baby boomers were corrupted by Elvis and The Beatles. With Generation X it was Mtv, then Millennials and Youtube. But do these claims come from hard data, or are they a collection of vague constellation-like assumptions about what we supposedly all know?

In books and articles on the subject, a lot of numbers are thrown around to try to prove far-fetched conclusions. Some features are consistent: conflating younger age groups with older ones, and blurring lines between suggestive (but mainstream) material with adult content. I'll give some examples.

In November 2010, Claire Perry, a British MP, spoke in Parliament on internet porn and how she felt government should address it.[i] The same month, the Sunday Times devoted several pages and a magazine spread to the topic.[ii]

What did Perry's claims include? One was that 60 per cent of nine- to nineteen-year-olds had found porn online. Ages nine to nineteen? That's a wide range. It includes people who are over the UK age of consent (sixteen plus) as well as those old enough to appear in pornography (eighteen plus). But the statement gives the impression that the majority of nine-year-olds are trawling naughty websites. If Perry's vague statistic were broken down by age, it would skew – heavily – towards the older end.

Another asserted '15 per cent of 12- to 17-year-olds have purposefully looked at X-rated material online.' Really? Funny, because you could also say that 15 per cent of 12- to 17-year-olds actually *are* 17. Stating that people over the UK age of consent may be looking at porn gives a different impression from implying a bunch of 12-year-olds are doing it.

From the same study, some vague definitions: '70 per cent of 15- to 17-year-old internet users accidentally view pornography "very" or "somewhat" often.' What counts as 'very often' varies from person to person, but none of us will be any the wiser, since the report doesn't define this.[iii]

Perry also claimed: 'A third of our British 10-year-olds have viewed pornography on the internet,' which would be worrying if it were true. But the figure is from Psychologies magazine's 'Put Porn In Its Place' campaign.[iv] Despite its name, Psychologies is not a peer-reviewed academic journal, but a mass market magazine like GQ or Cosmo. The articles were written by Decca Aitkenhead, a lifestyle columnist, not a researcher or science journalist.

The data were collected from a single year of boys at a single school in London. A small study population is not representative of children in general. More importantly, the poll was not of 10-year-olds and their habits. Rather, it was of 16-year-olds, and their memory of the first age at which they saw porn. See the difference? A study that relies people recalling an event a third of their lives ago will be riddled with errors. The study doesn't acknowledge this. In short, it's neither credible nor reliable.

Claire Perry's comments came one day after an event she attended at the Houses of Parliament, 'The Harm that Pornography Does; Its Effects on Adults and Children and the Need for Regulatory Reform.' The event was organised by Safermedia, whose co-chair, Miranda Suit, quotes a report also cited in the Sunday Times Magazine feature. The article mentions 'new research into the social costs of pornography from the Witherspoon Institute in America.'

Looking deeper, the 'research' turns out to be The Social Costs of Pornography: A Collection of Papers.[v] It includes contributions from Patrick Fagan from the Family Research Council, a far-right American lobbying organisation. As the Southern Poverty Law Center notes, "The FRC often makes false claims about the LGBT community based on discredited research and junk science." Is this who UK politicians should be working with?

Fagan also works with the Heritage Foundation, the think-tank that were architects of the Reagan administration's covert Cold War operations, and were active supporters of George W Bush's international policy. The Heritage Foundation has links to white supremacy defenders like Jason Richwine. Fagan's other recent papers mentioned on the Witherspoon site include 'Virgins Make the Best Valentines' and 'Why Congress Should Ignore Radical Feminist Opposition to Marriage.' Again: are these the people who should be one or two degrees of separation from UK government policymakers?

The Social Costs of Pornography admits their evidence is thin: 'The few statistics available about the use of pornography by children and adolescents are even more difficult to assess than those concerning adults ... Nevertheless, there can be no doubt that children and adolescents are far more exposed to pornography via the internet than they ever have been before.' How is it possible to make sweeping conclusions when there are no data?

It reflects again: 'But is there evidence that this exposure is harmful to children? For some people, no more evidence is needed.' This in spite of failing to produce even one study showing a cause-and-effect relationship. You'll excuse me for thinking a lot more evidence is needed!

Is any material from the Witherspoon report 'new'? No. The report is riddled with anachronisms. For instance, 'many people first encounter pornography on television in a hotel room'. Which the eagle-eyed will note is neither an internet phenomenon, nor a recent one, nor likely to be true for young people born after the 1970s. It's illustrated with a photo of porn star Jenna Jameson from fifteen years ago.

The aim of Witherspoon report is clear: 'political leaders should use the bully pulpit.' Celebrities are urged to apply pressure – pressure that looks like Justin Timberlake and Ashton Kutcher's "Real Men Don't Buy Girls" campaign (swiftly deprioritized once it emerged Kutcher was jetting party girls out to his suite in Vegas, behind then-wife Demi Moore's back). Again, the Witherspoon report admits the data do not support its cause: 'Some of the most important parts of our laws could not be justified if they had to hinge on a proof of material injuries.'

Like many think-tanks, Witherspoon has a strong bias. They also admit – repeatedly – that the evidence is insubstantial. UK policy is being spoon-fed to the government by some of America's most extreme conservatives, and people are lapping up everything they have to say without questioning where it comes from.

Right-wing think tanks are not the only source of dud stats, the left does it too. In 2009, the UK's Consultation on Sexualization of Young People was launched by Labour's then-Home Secretary Jacqui Smith, model Danielle Lloyd, and psychologist Linda Papadopoulos.

The review set its goal as seeing 'how sexualized images and messages may be affecting the development of children and young people and influencing cultural norms, and examines the evidence for a link between sexualization and violence.'

The report, released in 2010, contains no original research but is a review of various topics from violence to internet usage among children. Reviews have appeared before. One was by the American Psychological Association in 2007[vi]. Australia also released a similar report in 2008[vii]. These were well received, but the expectation was that later reports would take a fuller view of the context in which young people live. The 2009 Home Office report failed to do that.

The consultation is slickly produced, provides loads of policy recommendations, and is lacking in any qualities that would make good research. Conclusions are made in absence of citations. For example: 'Sexualized self-presentation could also mean that young people are exposing themselves to danger …' and '[I]t is widely accepted that exposure to content children are either emotionally or cognitively not mature enough for can have a negative impact.' No research is noted, no names mentioned, no paper referenced.

Other studies are quoted mainly of pornography and adults (which as the Witherspoon report noted, do not show clear connections). None refer to young people, or make a distinction between, say, a tween's crop top and hardcore porn.

The Home Office report leapfrogs across years, yet claims to be a reflection of current media culture. With sections analysing music videos from twenty years ago, the report not only feels – but is – out-dated. Technology has moved on, and citing technology obsolete before most teens were born is irrelevant.

Later, when a coalition government came into power in Britain, they also commissioned a review on sexualization. How did that compare to its predecessor? Did it present the balanced approach many people hoped for?

The report from 2011, Letting Children Be Children, was authored by Reg Bailey, head of the Mothers' Union, a Christian think-tank with no academic connections. But there were bigger problems than that:

- It did not summarise academic evidence regarding sexualization. It referred to previous consultations, but did not mention criticism of these.
- It did not gather evidence on effects of commercialization or sexualization, and ignored peer-reviewed research.
- It made recommendations, purportedly based on the results of the questionnaires and focus groups, however the responses did not support the changes suggested.

The report states: 'Insufficient evidence to prove conclusively there is harm to children does not mean that no harm exists.' So: none. In spite of the money and time invested, this is no better than any previous report.

The report summarises parent responses in a way that is patronising. For example: '... we believe that a truly family-friendly society would ... reinforce healthy norms for adults and children alike.' Yet nowhere are these 'norms' defined. And who on earth is 'we'? Added to which, in the section regarding proof of age to access internet erotica, mention of the potential usefulness of ID cards slips in – it's what some would consider a Orwellian nightmare.

The review recommends 'modest' clothing. But what is modest? I grew up in Gulf Coast Florida near the beach. 80-plus temperatures in winter were common. As you might imagine, bathing suits were perfectly acceptable in public. Seeing a woman of any age in shorts, a bikini top, and flip flops even off the beach was not only unremarkable, but unlikely to strike anyone as sexual. Adopting clothing more 'modest' than shorts and a tank top for little girls in August would be tantamount to child abuse. Transplant the same style of dressing to the UK, and the context is different. It looks inappropriate. It looks sexual, even if it isn't.

The sexualization discussion invokes 'children' as if they are a single group across the entire age spectrum. What's appropriate for a three-year-old? What's appropriate for someone fifteen years older? The way in which the results are presented is very misleading. On the question of advertising, the reviews claims that 40 per cent of parents had seen something they regarded as inappropriate or offensive. But flip it the other way around, and you get a different interpretation entirely: 60 per cent of parents had *not* seen anything they regarded as offensive in public advertising. Ever. That's actually a lot. And context is missing: the distinction between whether offensive adverts were seen once ever, or every day, is not made.

In other sections, the data disagree with the interpretation altogether. For example, the recommendation that lads' mags should be removed from places children might see them comes several pages before the data showing only 113 of 846 parents thought lads' mags were a concern. That's less than 15 per cent.

Elsewhere '72% [of parents] think the overall level of regulation for television programmes is about right.' Parents, it seems, can be off-message with the agenda ... and those opinions will likely be ignored, in service of a preferred outcome.

So, it was to no one's surprise when then-Prime Minister David Cameron announced he would be meeting with four big internet providers to discuss schemes for limiting access to porn.

Early reports confirmed that the approach being sought was 'opt-in' – objectionable content turned off unless you ask for it and prove your age. If you're a customer with BT, Sky, Talk Talk, or Virgin, should you expect to be sending them a copy of your passport in the not-so-distant future?

Interestingly, internet providers are not as on-board as reports suggested. One source at an ISP was quoted: 'We all want to make the internet as safe as possible, but we can't completely eliminate all risk – at least not without seriously affecting the vibrant and beneficial nature of the internet. The primary responsibility lies with the parents, who have a responsibility to supervise how their children use the internet.' [viii]

The main objections to ISP-level blocking are:

1. It will inadvertently block content that should not be blocked, such as sex education websites and medical information.

2. It may prevent access to vital resources for gay, trans, and otherwise questioning teens who find it difficult to get the support they need in their home communities.

3. It may be misused by people trying to have their competitors blocked.

4. There will be workarounds, making free access something that is

available to some people and not others: a two-tier internet, if you will.

The new UK Prime Minister Theresa May, from her former post as Home Secretary, has long endorsed internet controls dressing them up as "anti terrorism" instead of "protecting children." The results will be much the same.

As with the constellations we give names and stories to in the night sky, the time and place in which we observe something influences whether we think they're related. Taking a different perspective may show them not to be connected at all.

Looking at the results, a link between porn and negative outcomes turns out to be not supported. Consider widely-cited research by Neil Malamuth, whose work considers whether there is a causal link between adults who view pornography and sexual aggression.

Now, the difference between 'sexualizing' images aimed at children and actual pornography created for adults is apparent, and using such a study as a reference in a discussion of sexualization is suspect. When looking at how well a review makes its arguments, it's essential to ask whether the evidence being presented is not only accurate, but relevant.

But it would be almost impossible to conduct a study on direct effects of sexualizing images on children. You can't do it ethically, if at all.

In a comprehensive review of data from studies of adults, this simple question was raised: 'Hard-core pornography and sexual aggression: are there reliable effects and can we understand them?'[ix]

The conclusion was muted: 'We suggest that the way relatively aggressive men interpret and react to the same pornography may differ from that of nonaggressive men.' In other words, the pump is already primed in some people, and exposure enhances that tendency. But, for nonaggressive men, the same imagery did not incite negative thoughts.

So porn does not cause violence. If that's the case, how could it possibly make sense that other, less sexual and nonviolent things would?

One hallmark of drawing constellations is relying on anecdotes, or one-off stories. Canadian filmmaker Sharlene Azam's documentary *Oral Sex Is The New Goodnight Kiss* features girls as young as eleven years old talking about sex parties. What shocked the filmmaker the most was that '[t]he girls are almost always from good homes, but their parents are completely unaware.'[x]

The clips attracted a lot of attention, and were assumed to be representative of an entire generation. But a tiny group of middle class students is never going to be representative. And it's just as likely – as is often the case when a group of puberty-age kids get together – that being interviewed in a group leads to exaggeration to impress your peers. It's not a sociological phenomenon. It's just an anecdote.

There is a feeling that could be interpreted as contemptuous. A distaste for things of which feminists don't approve. What are we to make of books such as *Female Chauvinist Pigs* by Ariel Levy or *Living Dolls* by Natasha Walter? Books in which men are only mentioned insofar as they are the mildly amused directors of Girls Gone Wild or consumers of porn?

Such media tell a lot of stories, but do not offer any new analysis or substance. Important research is hinted at, but the data never broken down comprehensively. What the consumer gets instead are impressions, feelings … anecdotes.

Natasha Walter, in *Living Dolls*, spends most of the book preoccupied with the contents of other people's diaries. Jessica Valenti's *Full Frontal Feminism* is definitely about feminism, but the title seems sexed up for maximum shock effect. Kat Banyard, in *The Equality Illusion,* opens each chapter with 'a quasi fictional description of a girl or woman touched by each of the issues under discussion.'[xi] Quasi fictional? How about some facts?

While biased reports are silent on the matter of the real numbers in sex statistics, other wide-reaching studies show the large-scale trends.

The proportion of people who have had intercourse by the age of fifteen has risen among both sexes in Britain, but remains comfortably under 15 per cent. In a study from 1980 onward, the proportion of women losing their virginity by the age of sixteen showed a rise until the 1990s, when the numbers stabilised.[xii]

The author of the UK studies, Kaye Wellings, was quoted at a press conference as saying 'The selection of public health messages needs to be guided by epidemiological evidence rather than by myths and moral stances.'[xiii]

In the US, where most of the 'raunch culture' reporting occurs, the proportion of girls having sex before the age of fifteen has hardly changed from the late 1970s to today, and has *decreased* among boys.[xiv] The proportion of American high school students of any age who have had sex decreased in both boys and girls from 1991 to 2007.[xv] Access to sexualizing media is not correlated with more, or younger, sex.

Teen pregnancies are also going down. The *Journal of Adolescent Health* found teenage girls in 2012 were as likely to be sexually active as girls in 2007. 43 per cent of girls aged 15 to 19 said they'd ever had sex in 2007, compared with 45 per cent in 2012. But the birth rate plummeted: in 2007, 4.2 per cent of teenage girls in the US gave birth. In

2014, the rate was 2.4 per cent.

The faults of biased reviews might not be so clear had the Scottish Executive not commissioned a report that did more than just panic.

The Scottish Executive's External research on sexualized goods aimed at children begins with a literature review. The key earlier studies, from the American Psychological Association and the Australian Senate, are covered along with other relevant research. As well as highlighting these publications it considers their drawbacks. The Scottish review notes that '[s]uch accounts often present the sexualization ... as a relatively recent development, but it is by no means a new issue.'

Three main criticisms are made. The first is 'a lack of consistency and clarity about the meaning of sexualization' in other studies. The areas of concern are seldom defined, relying instead on assumptions to frame the debate, with many researchers using the same words to mean subtly different things.

Another problem is that 'much of the research suffers from methodological limitations that are characteristic of media effects research.' In general, media effects studies are conducted on small groups, which can bias the results but also be inapplicable to larger populations. Any laboratory study has to take that into account. It's likely that the attention subjects give things in the lab is pretty different from the attention they give in their natural surroundings – especially if they know they're going to be quizzed on it later.

Other reviews are criticised because the research 'rests on moral assumptions ... that are not adequately explained or justified.'

Parents saw similarities between their own and contemporary childhoods, about how they too had wanted to be 'grown up,' and the peer pressure they had experienced. One parent noted that 'nothing's changed really.'

Ideas about what was appropriate and what was not depended as much on subtext as on the content. One mother saw Playboy products as 'grooming' girls, but didn't object to her son's poster of model Jordan because Jordan was 'doing it for herself,' not aiming at children, and is a 'fellow single mother.'

They did not support the unsubstantiated statements made in books like *The Porning of America*[xvi] such as 'Bratz dolls fundamentally redefine girlhood – and make many parents feel as if porn is hunting their daughters.' The reactions of the parents were far more realistic. 'From an adult point of view then the Bratz doll is more overtly sexy but I don't think the kids see it that way ...' Rather than banning items they thought offensive, parents felt peer disapproval would suffice.

Much of the focus, it was agreed, was on girls. Parents tended to defend their own daughters as 'sensible,' eschewing 'inappropriate' clothing. And if they did wear it, it was for reasons other than sex: 'it's not like she's about to have sex with somebody because she's wearing thongs, it's just a look,' was one typical response. They tended to feel that in context, both they and their children did understand what was appropriate and what was not.

Both parents and children agreed that learning to make decisions about what was and what wasn't appropriate was part of growing up, and that parents help shape that. One girl commented 'I want something more grown up rather than just like Playboy Bunnies. I just thought it was a bit childish.'

Young people's active role was shown in their understanding of clothing and make-up having different meanings at different times. '[S]omething that might be sexy to someone else might not be to others.' They mentioned wearing more revealing clothing, or more make-up and accessories, to parties and discussed these as a way to have fun, that the point was to enjoy themselves rather than gain sexual attention.

Kids mentioned 'playing at' being older as part of growing up, when talking about themselves at a younger age. Girls trying out make-up or hairstyles and boys wearing hair gel in primary school were considered experiments in advance of secondary school. They did it to find out 'how much was too much' or how to 'get it right' before making those mistakes as a teenager. In other words, the children regarded those phases as a part of developing self-confidence and healthy sexuality.

It was considered appropriate not to display too much of the body or to attract attention through hair, make-up and accessories, so wearing products the young people considered 'sexual' made the participants uncomfortable. One concern by the girls was the risk of appearing too much older and of having their reputations misjudged.

There is a lot of conjecture about sexualization. But there is no evidence to justify the grim and worrying pictures of youth gone wild. Responsible research shows parents and children aware of the dangers of too much too soon. Most importantly: kids are astute judges of what is and is not appropriate. And the 'secondary effects' trumpeted by the left and the right? Do not exist.

This issue is a well-trod path with a predictable outcome, and demonstrates how biased polls are used to push bad agendas by shadowy interests. It is a pattern that happens over and over. Back in 1970, president Lyndon Johnson set up a US commission to examine the effects of pornography. One of its stated aims was to study '[t]he effects of such material, particularly on youth, and their relationship to crime and other antisocial conduct.'

The Report of the Commission on Obscenity and Pornography concluded that 'empirical investigation provided no evidence that exposure to or use of explicit sexual materials plays a significant role in the causation of social or individual harm.'

Unfortunately by the time the report was released, the US had a new president, Richard Nixon. Rather than evaluate the evidence on its merit, Nixon released a statement declaring, 'I have evaluated that report and categorically reject its morally bankrupt conclusions.'[xvii]

The Senate backed Nixon's statement over the facts, voting 60–5 to support the president's opinion (thirty-four senators abstained from voting). Politics, for neither the first nor the last time, prevailed over truth.

CHAPTER 2

Did You Know...

- *Strip clubs are not linked to violent crimes*
- *Porn use is not linked to violent crimes*
- *The most-quoted studies claiming they are contain fatal flaws*
- *Poorly designed research often tries to look like real statistics*

When confronted with things – such as statistical analysis – where the details are obscure, it can hard to tell the real from the fake. We look to trusted guides to act as translators to the layman. Official translators might include advisors to the government; unofficial ones include people in the media.

Even trusted guides can be fooled by reports that, to the untrained eye, look real. Such reports might use science-y terminology, or cite dodgy sources without properly examining the data.

This is even more likely to happen when talking about subjects that inspire strong emotional reactions. If the results seem like something we already assume, or fear, to be true, they are more likely to be accepted without close examination.

The borough of Camden in north London is a vibrant and diverse quarter of the city boasting almost 2000 pubs, 130 licensed entertainment venues, and seven lap dancing clubs.

Spearmint Rhino may look like any of the similar clubs in the area. In fact it's been the epicentre of controversy since it opened. Not only was it one of the first establishments granted an all-nude licence in the 1990s, it paved the way for identical clubs around the UK.

Spearmint Rhino was notable not only for full nudity but also for its style. It gained a reputation for having a less seedy atmosphere than previous clubs in Soho. Comfortable leather chairs curl around customers who patronised Britain's first all-nude strip club. The topless dancers at Stringfellows were modest titillation by comparison. Spearmint Rhino's arrival signalled a new era of adult entertainment in the capital.

Customers responded by making lap dancing the talk of the town. 'Table dancing has moved into the mainstream,' wrote Ben Flanagan in the Observer. 'The clubs, previously perceived as sleazy and hostile, are now seen as ideal venues for a corporate night out or a bit of celebrity-spotting.'

So when a 2003 study claimed a 50 per cent rise in rapes in areas surrounding lap dancing clubs, people were aghast. Rape isn't some indistinct 'secondary effect' like sexualization, it is a primary one. Even worse, reports suggested this was three times the national average. As a statistic it sounded shocking - but was it true?

It turns out this widely quoted study is a clear example of misuse of statistics. Regardless, it is still reported – even years after its major errors and incorrect conclusions were pointed out.

The report that sparked the headlines, 'Lap Dancing and Striptease in the Borough of Camden' was produced by Lilith R&D, part of the Eaves For Women charity.

The stated aim of Lilith was, according to its website, is 'to eliminate all aspects of violence against women.' A worthy ideal and important issue. But it doesn't necessarily equal good science.

The first flaw in the report is that their basic arithmetic is wrong.

According to the report, rapes in Camden had been on the rise since 1999. The number reported in 1999 in the borough was 72 rapes. By 2000 it was 88, 2001 had 91 and for 2002, the number of reported rapes in Camden was 96.

If you look at only the numbers, the difference from 1999 to 2002 is 24 rapes. But that's a 33 per cent increase – not 50 per cent. A basic error, and one that was surprisingly resistant to being corrected. It was only years later, in 2008, that the Guardian reported this elementary miscalculation[xviii]. The original claim of 50 per cent is still reported without being corrected.[xix]

Even with the arithmetic right, the increase *wasn't* 33 per cent because the population changed. The number may rise from year to year, but if the population is going up as well, the rate might not be changing at all. Using rates, rather than raw numbers, is one useful way to distinguish real statistics from nonsense results.

Imagine, for instance, if a paper claimed London has ten times as many Chinese restaurants than it did a hundred years ago, but didn't report the relative populations for those years. You wouldn't think much of the numbers. Of course the raw number would have gone up – the population got a lot bigger from 1917 to 2017. Without context, the numbers don't mean anything.

You don't have to be a London native to know the population is going up. It's on the rise in Camden. But is it going up enough to make the rate of rapes look different from the number? Let's see.

For the year 1999, we have 72 rapes reported in Camden and – according to National Statistics – a population of 195,700 people.

To determine how many rapes occurred per 100,000 residents, we divide the number of rapes by the total population. Then we multiply by 100,000:

$$72 \div 195,700 \times 100,000 = 36.8$$

In 1999, there were 36.8 reported rapes for every 100,000 residents of Camden. Performing the same rate calculation for the year 2000, when the population was 202,800 and the number of rapes 88, gives us a rate of 43.4.

Calculating the change in rate from one year to the next gives us the percentage change, be it a rise or a fall. The change in rate from 1999 to 2000, or the change from 36.8 to 43.4, is a 17.9 per cent rise.

That is considerably different from 50 per cent – about a third of what was claimed. So the rate (which is what counts) of rapes in Camden did not go up by 50 per cent after the lap dancing clubs opened. If you include the even more modest increases in 2001 and 2002, you still come up with a result that is nowhere close to the Lilith report's original claim. The combined change from 1999 to 2002 is a rate increase of 26.9 per cent.

But the story doesn't end there.

Context is important. Rapes might go up one year, or two, or three … and they might fall the next. You can't tell from one year, or two, or even three what is happening on a long-term scale. There are fluctuations that can mask the overall trend. The more data we have to analyse, the more accurate the results. The more accurate the results, the more informed the reporting.

It is also important to find out whether the rate was a one-off, or whether the rise implied in the Lilith report was sustained. So let's calculate rates, but this time for a longer timespan. We know that between 1999 and 2000 the rate of reported rapes in Camden rose. But did the trend continue? Have a look at the results:

Year	Rapes	Population	Rate per 100k	% change
1999	72	195,700	36.8	n/a
2000	88	202,800	43.4	+17.9
2001	91	202,600	44.9	+3.5
2002	96	205,700	46.7	+3.9
2003	71	207,700	34.2	-26.8
2004	52	212,800	24.4	-28.5
2005	68	218,400	31.1	+27.4
2006	67	221,500	30.2	-2.8
2007	70	223,900	31.3	+3.4
2008	41	226,500	18.1	-42.1

The change in rates fluctuates a lot year-to-year. So much so that between 2007 and 2008, it went *down* by over 40 per cent. Surprised? Actually, that's a feature of dealing with small numbers. Because the event is uncommon, a few incidents either way have more power to change the trend.

If we graph the rates, we can see if the trend is rising, falling, or staying the same. The years covered in the Lilith study are highlighted in red:

Rapes per 100,000 in Camden, 1999–2008

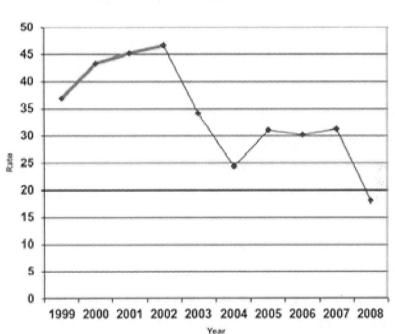

We see that for the ten years 1999–2008, the trend is falling, not rising. During this time the clubs did not close, nor did they suffer a loss in patronage.

The original paper also lacks a control population, with which to compare the results. Controls are populations where the thing you want to test doesn't exist, for comparison purposes. The report makes comparisons between Camden, Westminster and Islington, all of which contain lap dancing clubs. As far as control populations go, that's no good: you need somewhere where there are *no* clubs.

Without doing this, it's impossible to say whether any trend was locally concentrated or happening everywhere regardless of strip clubs.

Lambeth has a somewhat larger population than Camden and similar make-up in terms of ethnic origin. It contains no lap dancing clubs at all. Islington has a somewhat smaller population than the other two boroughs and has two venues licensed for fully nude lap dancing. And since these statistics are also available for the entire country, let's throw that in too. After all, the original claim was that Camden's rape stats were three times the national average.

Now, the graph of those data. Again, the years covered by the Lilith paper for Camden are highlighted in red:

Rapes per 100,000 in Camden, 1999–2008

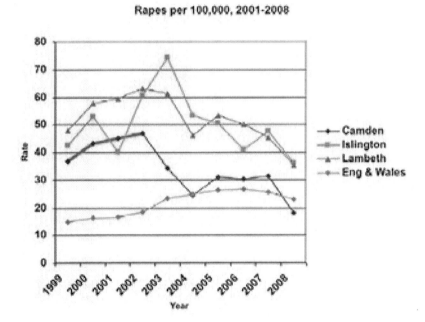

This graph changes the picture considerably. Boroughs with fewer or no clubs had higher rates than Camden's. All three boroughs have decreased over time, as well, which is why it pays to look at the longer trend rather than cherry-picking a few years.

Apart from the early 2000s peak, Camden's numbers are close to the overall rate for England and Wales, and sometimes even below it. This is a far cry from the 'three times the national average' claimed by the Lilith report.

It is because rape is such a serious crime that researchers must be at least as rigorous in their analysis as they would with other events. Otherwise, it's not real analysis. It's throwing numbers around without context. It's producing reports that look and feel like real research without the methodology to back them up. Scientists call this "cargo cult" research.

To avoid becoming cargo cult scientists, Richard Feynman said researchers must be willing to question results, and investigate possible flaws in a theory. 'We've learned from experience that the truth will come out,' Feynman said. 'Although you may gain some temporary fame and excitement, you will not gain a good reputation as a scientist if you haven't tried to be very careful in this kind of work.'

To a layperson, cargo cult science and real science look similar in that they contain numbers and try to come to some sort of conclusion. But even if the Lilith report had managed to get its arithmetic correct, there still would have been clues that the look and feel of real research was being imitated, and the content wasn't up to scratch.

It's pretty easy to pick out cargo cult research, because usually:

1. **It shows only raw numbers, not a rate.** Rates are the bread and butter of incidence statistics, and a written-in-stone requirement of any report dealing with a population group. How do I know? Because I used to write papers reporting children's cancer rates. No rate = no paper. If one year's incidence is being compared to another, expect to see rates, not raw numbers.

2. **It doesn't show a long-term trend.** In the Lilith report, a small number of years were reported. Rapes before the lap dancing clubs arrived weren't shown, so they couldn't be compared. Rapes more than two years after weren't shown, so it was impossible to see if the trend was real.

3. **It doesn't use a control group.** Control groups, when it comes to population statistics like these, are hard. I get it. There's no Truman Show bubble world kept somewhere for us to compare everything to. But, as we say where I come from, hard cheese. You make do. Mention was made in the report of other boroughs (such as Islington) that have lap dancing clubs, but crimes in areas of London without lap dancing clubs were not even mentioned so no comparison could be made. The rest of the country was not considered.

4. **It makes a causal connection without evidence**, and doesn't consider other factors. Statisticians talk about 'confounders' – the other factors that can affect your results. On the basis of a short-term miscalculated trend, a cause-and-effect relationship is claimed between lap dancing and rape. However, this does

not take into account the types of rapes reported, any possible correlation with crime hotspots within the borough, or any other possible contributing factors.

As the old computing saying goes, "garbage in, garbage out." You can't expect a good result when the data are poor. The Lilith report on Camden shows how bad data collection and lazy analysis produce misleading and incorrect results.

You might wonder why the Lilith report chose Camden at all. According to the introduction, it was because 'Lilith and Eaves believe that Camden's opinion and acts carry great weight with other London boroughs.' In other words, not because Camden is a high risk area, but because it's popular and trendy. That's a stupid reason to choose it.

There are other places where the opening of lap dancing clubs does also seem to correlate with a reduction in rape. One of these is the small city of Newquay, in Cornwall.

In 2010, the paper Newquay Voice obtained Devon and Cornwall Constabulary's figures of sexual assaults.[xx] They found that the total number of recorded sexual assaults (including rapes) in and around Newquay peaked at 71 in 2005, the year before Newquay's first lap dance club opened. In 2006, the year following its opening, the number fell to 51.

In 2007, when the town's second lap dancing venue opened, the total number of recorded sexual assaults fell again to 41, then dropped to 27 in 2008 when a third lap dancing club opened. In 2009, the number rose slightly but the total of 33 offences is still less than half the 2005 total. Here are the incidence rate calculations (using mid-year population levels for the council of Restormel, where Newquay is located):

Year	Population	Rapes	Rate per 100k
2005	100,400	71	70.7
2006	101,000	51	50.5
2007	101,900	41	40.2
2008	102,500	27	26.3
2009	103,100	33	32.0

The rate goes *down* every year except the last.

In spite of this, in 2012 a police inspector write a letter to the local newspaper claiming the clubs caused rape. A Freedom of Information request was made asking to see his evidence. Inspector Ian Drummond-Smith was forced to admit to the BBC "I cannot prove any link, nor did I claim to prove any link."

The Cornwall data reinforces the same thing the statistics from Camden show: that lap dancing does not correlate with a higher occurrence of rape. And if there is no rise, then it is impossible to claim lap dancing 'causes' rape.

In fact, the question of what effect adult services have on local crime has been studied so thoroughly that there can now be studies of the studies, or what statisticians call 'meta-analysis.' A meta-analysis, or pooled analysis, combines the results of published studies by many different groups in order to arrive at an overall conclusion.

A meta-analysis examined 110 papers that claimed adult businesses increased crime rates.[xxi] What they found was startling. In fact, 73 per cent of the papers were records of political discussions, not actual studies at all. Removing these and anecdotal reports, the authors were left with twenty-nine studies. In the papers that did not contain flaws, there was no correlation between any adult-oriented business and any negative effect. Of the ten most frequently cited papers, not one met the minimum standards for good research.[xxii]

The theory that adult entertainment causes 'secondary effects' comes straight from radical 1970s feminists who believed that all heterosexual sex was rape. As time went on, they accrued the money and academic positions to allow them to craft bogus studies to fit their assumptions.

Poor research starts from an assumed position, and any data falling outside of that position are ignored. The writers are biased and try to make the numbers to fit their preconceived notions rather than what it actually is.

We can see this on the first page of the Lilith report with statements like: 'This "fast fantasy" approach is demeaning and insulting to women … Lap dance [is] not going away without a fight.'

It is clear the writers of the report have a particular agenda – prohibiting adult entertainment. Claiming the methods of science, without buying in to the philosophy of how and why they work, is unethical. If you don't play by the same rules, you can't use the same tools.

The tone of the report is so attached to its assumptions that it does not address several other problems.

Let's pretend for a moment their assumption was correct. If so, why would the rapes occur in Camden? The area containing the clubs is a small corner of a much larger borough bordering other parts of London, with customers from elsewhere. You might expect such a famous venue to have customers from elsewhere in the country. There is no evidence that the crimes would be committed in Camden. Such possible confounding factors are not addressed in the study.

The paper also implies that the rapes are stranger rapes. That seeing naked women causes men to stand in alleys outside waiting to rape. A Home Office report analysing relationships between victims and offenders notes that for rapes, strangers are the perpetrators in only 17 per cent of UK cases, and that 75 per cent of reported rapes occur either in the victim's home or in the perpetrator's.

The claim made in the Lilith report – that the number of reported rapes is rising – is not true. It was not true in 2003, it continues not to be true, yet the myth that rapes rise 50 per cent after lap dancing clubs opened in Camden is still reported. Why?

In 'Feminism, Moralism, and Pornography,' Ellen Willis discusses feminists who seek to promote 'erotica' while condemning 'pornography.' More than a couple of recent high-profile feminist memoirs have done exactly this. Tina Fey and Lena Dunham, to name but a couple. It's kind of like the women who would go to tongue-in-cheek 'burlesque' performances, but shriek at the thought of entering a strip club. What's the difference, exactly? How is it possible to be a fan of one, and despise the other?

Willis points out that this kind of hypocrisy appeals to an idealized version of what kind of sex people should want rather than what actually sexually arouses them. In this view, vintage pin-ups = good, trashy lingerie = bad. Dita Von Teese is an artist, but the dancers in the local strip club are sad dregs of humanity. Suicide Girls? Approved. Playboy? Evil. And so on. 'In practice, attempts to sort out good erotica from bad porn inevitably comes down to "What turns me on is erotica; what turns you on is pornographic."'

Media coverage tends to be either smutty or judgmental because that's easier to write. Journalists are prone to relying on self-appointed anti-obscenity crusaders who don't acknowledge opposing viewpoints. What people hear in mainstream media is limited to studies made by people with an agenda against adult entertainment.

Many anti-porn arguments rely not on what is testable and verifiable, but are based instead on the untestable and unverifiable opinions of highly biased, self-selecting interviewees.

Consider the writing of anti-porn crusader Gail Dines. Dines, who teaches women's studies at Wheelock College in Massachusetts, is a founding member of Stop Porn Culture. Using press releases and conferences, Stop Porn Culture tries to whip up media frenzies that are high on emotion and thin on firm evidence.

Dines' first book claims to report the truth about porn, but is virtually free of objective analysis. Rather than design a study that would pass peer review, Dines relies heavily on reporting people's 'gut feelings' in response to being shown a montage 1970s-era anti-pornography material[xxiii].

By basing work on feedback from her conferences, Dines introduces a lot of bias. The audience is self-selecting (and therefore biased) since the paying attendees already have some sympathy to Dines' opinions. Dines herself admits the material is skewed.

The result is a carefully curated set of responses from people whose opinions were already decided. In scientific contexts, this would be unpublishable. But media publicises this, overshadowing the rational, well-designed research. It's the fast food of academia, and reporters fall for it every time.

In Pornland[xxiv], Dines continued in the same vein, arguing adult material affects relationships. But Dines does not conduct studies on couples and their use of porn, instead relying on 'a compelling, close reading of the imagery and narrative content of magazines, videos, and marketing materials.' In other words: she interviewed no one. *The only data comes from her.* She includes anecdotes about how she feels.

Elsewhere, Dines interviewed men in prison who had raped children. Every one of them was a habitual user of child pornography. The problem with Dines' interviews is that she got the 'cause' and 'effect' parts the wrong way around. This is a known as the Texas sharpshooter fallacy and it's a common tactic in fraudulent research. The Texas sharpshooter fires his rounds at the side of the wall, and then goes along painting targets around where the shots landed. Surprise surprise, he gets a bullseye every time!

The Texas sharpshooter approach would be like studying lung cancer patients, discovering the vast majority had smoked, and concluding that lung cancer causes smoking. Choosing a group of convicted child sex offenders, then finding that they had viewed child pornography is Texas sharpshooting at its finest. Dines' interviews tell us nothing about the nature either of pornography or of crimes against children. What it tells us a lot about is the interviewer's lack of understanding about how evidence works. But then, Texas sharpshooters have a much lower success rate when they put up a target before they fire their guns.

People who object to porn love to talk about the money: erotica is a profitable business, and online content alone is estimated to generate $3000 every minute in sales.[xxv] That sure sounds like a lot. However, implying that because something is profitable, it must be bad is a strange claim to make. After all, food is also profitable. That doesn't make it bad for you. When was the last time you ate something that was completely free?

Just because erotica can be a commodity does not put it at odds with human desire. After all, if it did not arouse, it would not sell.

As far as commodities go, well, porn is only a piece of the entire entertainment pie. While most reports claim the adult industry is big and ubiquitous, most of them also fail to compare it to anything else. On RedTube (a popular erotic video site), of the many videos available there are only 120 that have attracted over 1 million viewers. At first glance, that seems like a lot.

Until you compare it with non-sex videos, that is. On YouTube, for the keyword 'kitten' there are over 100 videos that have over 1 million viewers. About 500 videos tagged 'Justin Bieber' have achieved the same status. Even Lego gets more videos with high view counts than on the entire RedTube site.[xxvi]

The money in adult entertainment is dwarfed by the turnover of all other entertainment. In the Premier League of English soccer, players have an average salary of £1.46 million each. Porn stars make about £190–£600 per film. Each of the six principal cast members of Friends made $1 million per episode in its final series. There has never been a porn film with a total budget of $1,000,000 … much less a cast budget of $6 million plus. Hugh Hefner reportedly planned to buy back Playboy, the largest adult entertainment company, in a deal worth $200,000,000 – or less than a tenth of Facebook's value.

Critics of porn also talk about the content of the product as if that reveals how it was made. Assuming that because the actors on screen are doing one thing – a man being whipped by a dominatrix, say, or a woman engaging in group sex – that this is the relationship off screen is baffling. They're actors. They're acting.

'Pornography has a central role in actualizing this system of subordination in the contemporary West, beginning with the conditions of its production,' claimed Catharine MacKinnon.[xxvii] Evidence she gave to support this statement? None.

There's a huge difference between acting and reality. Using MacKinnon's logic would be like claiming Bambi Woods, star of the classic 70s porno Debbie Does Dallas, actually had sex with all 928,000 residents of Dallas in 1978. Of course she didn't!

Erotica is fantasy. It is not documentary. A porn actor playing a submissive in one film might turn up as a cuckolding wife in another. No one assumes mainstream actors are exactly like the people they play. It would be silly to think Ben Affleck really was Batman, or that Keanu Reeves is actually capable of walking through walls like he did in the Matrix trilogy, but even people who should know better assume what they see in porn is literal reality.

Being concerned about how porn is made is a good idea. It is like being concerned about how your clothes are made. It is impossible to tell from looking at a T-shirt whether it was made in ethical conditions, or whether people were exploited in making it. A conservative long-sleeved blouse might come from a sweatshop. A simple tee could come from a factory where everyone was treated and paid well. The appearance of the finished product is no indication of what went into it. You would only know the conditions involved by doing your homework.

Consider Linda Lovelace, star of Deep Throat, the first mainstream porn hit. The film is prim by today's standards. It later came out that Lovelace was coerced and abused throughout her career. Contrast that with one of porn's recent stars, Sasha Grey. Grey was well known for her gonzo humiliation scenes, but her career owed nothing to pimps or abusers. There is zero indication in the content of either film to tell you which woman was abused and which woman wasn't.

It's acting, after all – what's on screen is not the way the people are in real life. Hard-core kink scenes can have entirely willing, consenting participants. 'Vanilla' soft porn could include people who are coerced, trafficked, or abused. Making conclusions based on the plot is silly, and no way to be an informed consumer.

There are already strong laws in place concerning who can appear in porn and how the business operates. US regulations on proof of age and industry medical standards are adhered to widely. If the opponents got their way and all porn was illegal, there would be little incentive for filmmakers to make or keep proof of age and consent, since such evidence would be used against them as evidence of crime. As has happened so often when something is prohibited, the legitimate producers would give way to the black market. The porn business has come a long way since the days of Linda Lovelace; let's not send it back there.

Many sources keep the focus of the discussion on people's fears about what might happen in some dystopian future, rather than on data from right now. Partly, this reflects an unease people have with new technology.

Reliable studies contradict any connection between porn and violence. 'There's absolutely no evidence that pornography does anything negative' says Milton Diamond, a professor at the University of Hawaii in an interview in Scientific American.[xxviii] 'It's a moral issue, not a factual issue.'

Studies by Aleksandar Štulhofer at the University of Zagreb have examined sexual compulsivity. One surveyed 650 men about pornography and their sex lives.[xxix] Results showed that viewers of pornography were as sexually satisfied as non-users. Both groups reported the same levels of intimacy in their relationships. They even shared the same range of sexual experiences.

In 2007, a survey on sexist tendencies was included in mail-order porn deliveries sent out across Australia. Responses from 1023 people showed that the amount of pornography they consumed was not correlated with negative attitudes toward women. Other factors, such as level of education and political tendencies, were more indicative of whether someone was sexist.[xxx]

Simon-Louis Lajeunesse is a professor at the University of Montreal who attempted to design a study of the impact of pornography on the sexuality of men, and how it shapes their perception of men and women. In a prospective study of 20 students, Lajeunesse found most of the men questioned sought out porn by the age of ten, when they become sexually curious. He also found they quickly discarded what they didn't like and things they found offensive. As adults, they looked for content that was compatible with their sex preferences.[xxxi]

All of Lajeunesse's subjects supported gender equality and felt victimised by criticism of pornography. His subjects reiterated that they wanted real women, not fantasy women. Watching porn did not change their tastes or relationship goals in any significant way. If pornography had the impact that many claim it has, you would just have to show heterosexual films to a homosexual man to change his sexual orientation. These intriguing observations, however, never fully developed as a research project, since Lajeunesse was unable find control subjects: young men who had not seen any porn.

Rates of rapes and sexual assault in the US are now at their lowest levels since the 1960s. Studies show that in the US, the introduction of internet access in US states corresponded with a decrease in rape (and no effect on other violent crimes). A 10 per cent increase in online access corresponded with a 7.3 per cent decrease in reported rapes.[xxxii] States slowest to adopt internet technology experienced a 53 per cent increase in rape incidence, whereas the states with the most access experienced a 27 per cent drop in the number of reported rapes. And the effects remain even when taking into account confounders such as alcohol use, law enforcement, income, employment, and population density.[xxxiii]

There is an interesting similarity between such results and research into violence. When a violent film is released at the cinema, crime rates – surprisingly enough – go down. Apparently movie violence doesn't increase real-life violence after all. The theory is that people disposed to violence like watching violent films, and given the choice between the latest shoot 'em up thriller and going out to commit crime, plump for the popcorn option.[xxxiv]

Studies show sexual criminals tend to be exposed to pornographic materials at a later age than non-criminals. In 1992 Richard Green of Imperial College wrote how patients in a sex offenders' clinic cited pornography as a tool to keep desires within the confines of their imagination.[xxxv] Pornography seems to be protective, perhaps because exposure correlates with lower levels of sexual repression, a potential rape risk factor.

Does this prove that, in fact, internet access and violent films actually reduce rape and violent crime? No, not really. Not yet. There would have to be a lot more research – from many more angles – to even begin to support such a claim. Again, correlation is not causation. Bu they do *disprove* a common assumption.

The data do not support the claim that porn incites violence. Porn's gone up, rape's fallen. As the internet has increased access to erotic material, the effect has not only been enhanced, but measurable. So either they're related but in the opposite way to how people expect, or they're not actually related at all. Either way, it's a far better outcome than anyone predicted.

There is a shadowy other in the discussion about online lives. That is the availability not only of mainstream erotica, but also the spectre of extreme material. It raises the question of who might access such things, and whether this results in violence against other people.

As unpleasant as violent pornography may be to most people, it is not in any way common sense to assume that those that watching it want to participate. We all fantasise about things we would never do in real life. Some fantasies are innocent, some less so. It's human nature. We must be held responsible for our actions, not our thoughts.

The content of edgy porn is proscribed in other ways as well. In January 2012, Michael Peacock stood trial for distributing allegedly 'obscene' DVDs, containing scenes of men fisting each other, urination, and bondage. The rather delicious irony is that not only are such acts relatively common in the "kinky" community (I've even written about all of them), they're perfectly legal for consenting adults to participate in and watch in person. The outcome of the trial was therefore important, because if the material Peacock is alleged to have distributed was judged 'not obscene,' porn produced and sold in the UK will theoretically be free to contain scenes of fisting and urination.

The Obscene Publications Act 1959, under which Peacock was

prosecuted, aims to judge content on whether it is liable to "deprave and corrupt". One of the interesting things about the interpretation of this law is that while it isn't written to single out sex acts specifically, the acts considered to be prosecutable under the Obscene Publications Act are all of a sexual nature. So, for instance, you might consider images of a man being beaten and shot to be obscene if published in a newspaper; yet this happens with some frequency and the law is not invoked against it. Watching jumpy video of Gaddafi's last moments is fine; consensual watersports is not.

Rather wonderfully, the jury came back with a verdict of Not Guilty, unanimously, on all counts after about a tea-break's worth of deliberation.

For those who value personal liberty, it was a win. It also revealed a lot about the state of how the public views sex today. It's that perhaps we are finally beginning to become comfortable with the idea of consent, the notion that one does not have to practice a particular sexual kink or orientation to not condemn it, and that people who approach an escort who goes by the handle "Sleazy Michael" and rent or buy DVDs from him are possibly, just possibly, not being blindsided by the nature of their content.

It was only after the trial began that I realized the defendant, Michael Peacock, was someone I know. In my opinion he is a nice person who is genuinely enthusiastic about his work and his clients. In short, the best kind of escort. A really top bloke. And brave too. The thought that he corrupts or defiles anyone who doesn't want said treatment is frankly ridiculous.

In general, men who are sex workers are inconvenient to anti-sex work campaigners. Their existence makes the 'porn and prostitution are violence against women' line demonstrably untrue, and goes against the neat categorizations of men as always predators and women as always victims. So what do the majority of biased researchers do? Ignore them altogether, unfortunately – leaving the bulk of what we know about men who have sex with men (money involved or not) to HIV research alone.

Nevertheless, Peacock's trial does reveal a line of thinking that is pervasive when it comes to sex. The sexualization debate is entirely built on the erroneous assumption that if suggestive material wasn't available, people would never become curious about sex. Someone who distributes images of consenting adults engaging in perfectly legal acts is targeted simply because it is Big Bad Sex.

Worryingly, criminals are happy to jump on excuses like 'porn made me do it' and 'sexual addiction changed me' instead of admitting their own depravity. Dines and people like her provide the excuses murderers and rapists use to claim they're not really guilty.

Serial murderer Ted Bundy claimed a porn addiction made him do it, and this was repeated and reported as if gospel truth. Respected sex therapist Dr Marty Klein summarizes the problems with this. 'If convicted mass murderer Ted Bundy had said that watching Bill Cosby reruns motivated his awful crimes, he would have been dismissed as a deranged sociopath.'[xxxvi] Why give his porn claims any weight? Of course he wanted to reduce his own responsibility in these crimes ... he was facing death row.

In 2015, Tea Party activist Christian Hine was arrested for possessing child pornography. Hine's lawyers suggested that his "porn addiction" caused him to seek "harder" material to get his fix – that their client was a victim of evil, evil porn rather than an adult man with responsibility for his decision. A get out of jail free ploy, so that these men don't have to do any real soul-searching.

The evidence that porn does not cause violence is ample, but has yet to penetrate the news media. 'The cycle of addiction leads one way: towards ever harder material' claims Edward Marriott in the Guardian. As evidence he makes reference to 'the now-infamous Carnegie Mellon study of porn on the internet'.[xxxvii]

Unfortunately for Marriott, the study he mentions is a well-known hoax. 'Marketing Pornography on the Information Superhighway' was a high-profile piece that looked at Usenet groups.[xxxviii] Its shocking results were widely publicized – until Time magazine was forced to admit that it had all been made up. Academics whose names had been associated with the research were quick to distance themselves from it.[xxxix] It's pretty surprising for someone to know about that article and not know about it being discredited so publically, given the info is even noted on Wikipedia.

But misinformation, as it turns out, is not rare at all when the topic is sex.

CHAPTER 3

Did You Know...

• *Laws to "control" sex work put sex workers at more risk of danger*
• *Decriminalization, not legalization, offers the greatest safety*
• *There is a robust, well-funded industry of poor research profiting off of harm done to sex workers*

The first time I heard Michaela Hague's name was the day after she died.

It was my second year in Sheffield. I moved there in 2000 to start doctoral studies and lived in a converted church in the city center. The church had recently been renovated into student flats. It was clean, modern, and comfortable.

St George's Church was also right in the middle of the red light area.

The university literature had failed to mention that its grade-II listed showpiece of student accommodation was also a popular landmark with Sheffield's streetwalkers and kerb crawlers. I figured it out quickly enough, though. I had no inkling at the time that, just four years later, I too would be working in the sex industry.

It was not a bad place to live. The furtive clients who cruised the area rarely bothered residents. CCTV cameras, streetlights, and regular police cars added to a feeling of safety. During the day, St George's looked respectable and sedate. As one of the few people living in that area the sex trade didn't affect me; late-night student bars and noisy trams were more of a nuisance.

The area changed not long after, though. A TV documentary Life of Grime featured multiple episodes all within five minutes' walk of the church. Suddenly road blocks appeared to stop cars circling round the neighborhood. Women were moved off from the corners they usually worked. The street-based sex trade departed from the well-lit centre and relocated to the industrial areas around Corporation Street.

I was studying at the Medico-Legal Centre, where Sheffield's city mortuary shared space with the Forensic Pathology Department. It was in that mortuary I saw what I would come to associate most strongly with the effects of driving the streetwalkers away from St George's.

One morning I saw a postmortem that I still remember in excruciating detail. A woman was stabbed in a frenzied attack out past the dark underpasses of the Wicker, not far from Corporation Street. She lived long enough to give a partial description of her attacker but died in hospital. The victim was only twenty-five years old. I had turned twenty-six the night she died.

Michaela Hague was picked up by someone unknown, stabbed nineteen times, and left for dead. Her killer has never been found.

Michaela Hague was not only the victim of a depraved murderer. She was also a victim of a policy that is more concerned with exploiting prostitution myths than it is about helping women.

Before discussing how attitudes to sex work harm sex workers, let's take a trip into the not-so-distant past.

The brothels that flourished in the American West from the 1860s onwards were remarkably liberating for the women who worked there. Prostitutes enjoyed rights that mainstream feminism would secure only decades later. In an era when women were barred from most jobs and had no ownership rights, sex workers made the highest wages of all American women and could own property.

The average brothel worker earned from one to five dollars per trick. Many earned more in a single night than women in other jobs could get in a week. Sixty per cent of prostitutes in Helena, Montana, in the 1860s 'reported either personal wealth or property or both.' Prostitutes' average monthly income there was $233 – far higher than that of skilled tradesmen who earned $90 and 'white collar' men making $125 per month. The red-light district in Helena was 'women's business grounded in women's property and capital.'[xl] The average age of a prostitute in the Old West was twenty-three.[xli]

In the US in 1916, the average weekly wage for women in other occupations was $6.67. Most women were not permitted to work and earned nothing at all. Skilled male tradesmen earned $20 per week. Prostitutes earned between $30 and $50 per week. Some women achieved security by marrying well, but with no property rights, wives possessed little of their own. By contrast, women in the sex trade could live well on their own terms.[xlii] One lady of the time summed it up: 'Do you suppose I am going back to earn five or six dollars a week in a factory, and at that, never have a cent of it to spend for myself, when I can earn that amount any night, and often much more?'[xliii]

Brothel madams funded public works projects throughout the West. In Denver, madam Jennie Rogers paid for water services to the city. 'Diamond Jessie' Hayman gave food and clothing to thousands left homeless by San Francisco's 1906 earthquake. Lou Graham of Seattle, 'Queen of the Lava Beds,' helped fund the city's public school system. Anna Wilson, 'Queen of the Omaha Underworld,' bequeathed her mansion to the city. It became the region's first emergency hospital and infectious disease clinic.

Then there was 'Mammy' Pleasant. Born Mary Ellen, Pleasant escaped indentured servitude and became a successful madam in San Francisco. She worked with the Underground Railroad, moving people trapped in slave states to free territory, and was a financial supporter of revolutionary abolitionist John Brown. As well as investing in mining stock and making loans to the city's elite, Pleasant earned the moniker 'the mother of human rights in California' after filing a lawsuit to desegregate San Francisco's streetcars.

In Western courts sex workers challenged men who assaulted or robbed them, and frequently won. In half of such cases 'the judge or jury found for the female complainants.' A successful ratio even by today's standards. Blind eyes were turned when it was sensible to do so: there was 'a singular lack of legal and judicial concern with sexual commerce … [O]fficers of the law arrested no women for prostitution or keeping a disorderly house before 1886, even though the police court was located in the red-light district.' While most women had little recourse against violence, even in cases of marital rape, madams enlisted bodyguards to protect their employees.

This was not unique to the US West. As noted by Hallie Rubenhold, author of *Covent Garden Ladies*, late 18th century London was similar. Sex workers were part of the community: "there were no red-light districts, how prostitutes lived cheek-by-jowl with everyone else in their neighborhoods."

Also, it was a slice of freedom in a society where women had little. "Prostitution was the only way … a woman born into poverty could scale the heights and potentially even marry a man of title," Rubenhold notes. "Selling their bodies was one of the only means by which they could achieve some control over their lives, and in many cases, it was a far better option than marrying a man of their own social class and passing their days in poverty and endless childbirth."

Conditions for sex workers today vary widely. Some work in safety, others do not. Some earn a lot of money and others very little. In spite of the breadth of jobs that fall under the sex work umbrella, a tiny minority of worst case scenarios seem to the public more "realistic" – even when the data don't support that view. They are certainly the most written about, whether in the news or in books and on television.

Research from many people across several disciplines shows that the more someone is exposed to an idea, even if false, the less able they are to detect errors in reasoning. And so the pump is primed for sex workers to be consistently misrepresented. 'Familiarity is a heuristic,' says Gordon Pennycook of Yale University. 'If something is familiar, it's easier to process, and if it's easier to process, it feels right.' Even if it isn't.

Stereotypes of sex workers lead people to believe they all have chaotic, desperate lives. Until recently the UK government's website claimed: 'Most women involved in street-based prostitution are not there through choice ... Nearly all prostitutes are addicted to drugs or alcohol. Many of them have been trafficked into the country by criminals, and are held against their will. Many were abused as children, and many are homeless.'[xliv] There were no sources given for these statements – for the simple fact that they are wrong. (The false information has since been removed.)

Lamenting the narrow focus of most research, Laura Agustín notes '[t]he focus is usually on personal motivations, the morality of the buying-and-selling relationship, stigma, violence and disease prevention.'[xlv] Instead, we should think about sex work as real work, and protecting the people who do it as we would workers in any industry.

Is it dangerous? It can be. But sex work is statistically less dangerous than emergency services, military service, deep sea fishing, logging, and more. Whether one picks a career as a deep-sea fisherman or as a call girl, the potential income and danger are well publicized, and yet people sign up willingly. This is a choice everyone has the right to make for him or herself.

This was true in my case: my work as a call girl left time to look for science jobs, finish writing a doctoral thesis, and compete in rowing at a high level. Juggling all that with waitressing not only wouldn't have paid the bills, it wouldn't have left time to pursue a professional career.

But it wasn't only about convenience. As a non-EU migrant to the UK, the number of hours I could work were restricted to fifteen a week or fewer and outside of term time only. I couldn't be hired for a job if any qualified UK applicant walked in the door. Public assistance and welfare were off-limits. Sex work is an attractive job for migrants, many of whom are unable to access benefits in their adopted countries.

Many of the stock phrases about prostitution are wrong, easily disproven... and believed with almost religious fervor. Ever hear the one that claims '75 per cent of women in prostitution become involved when they are under the age of eighteen'? It's entirely incorrect.

In the UK, the breakdown is average age of twenty-one for streetwalkers, twenty-five for off-street and agency escorts, and nearly thirty-two for sauna sex workers.[xlvi] (Globally, numerous studies confirm streetwalkers represent a minority of sex workers – about 15% of all prostitution in most countries. Far more common are people working from home, in brothels, or visiting client premises.)

Ronald Weitzer[xlvii] found that escorts saw their work positively, while the brothel girls were satisfied and streetwalkers were mainly dissatisfied. 97 per cent of escorts surveyed reported an increase in self-esteem after they started sex work, compared with 50 per cent of Nevada brothel workers and 8 per cent of streetwalkers. Other studies confirm this – Dutch research shows similar results.[xlviii] In the US, 75 per cent of escorts felt their lives had improved since starting sex work, 25 per cent reported no change. No respondents said their lives were worse.[xlix] An Australian study found half considered their work as a 'major source of satisfaction'; 70 per cent said they would choose sex work again.[l] Regardless of circumstances or job satisfaction, though, all sex workers deserve equal rights.

On a day-to-day basis, sex workers are more likely to have a negative encounter with police than they are with a client. They are as likely to be raped by the police as helped by them. A 2012 study from the Young Women's Empowerment Project in Chicago found sex workers experienced seven times as much violence from police as they did from pimps. Demonizing sex workers and painting them as criminals makes them more vulnerable, and puts them in direct contact with more violence.

While having sex for money is legal in Britain, soliciting and loitering are not. As a result, prostitution crackdowns there target streetwalkers – the criminalized end of the sex work continuum. Evidence shows streetwalkers in the UK account for 5–20 per cent of all prostitutes – the remaining 80–95 per cent work in brothels, in massage parlours, or as escorts[li].

It is widely assumed that sex work promotes crime. One of the problems with data is teasing out the cause from the effect: is prostitution something that encourages local crime, or do streetwalkers happen to work to areas in which higher crime rates already exist? Are the people on the streets pushed into the margins when they get there, or does being marginalized force them to make suboptimal choices from what little is available?

You might expect the government to be interested in which came first in this chicken-or-egg situation but they are not. The Home Office report *Kerb-Crawling, Prostitution and Multi-Agency Policing*[lii] looked at a police crackdown in Finsbury Park, London. Its first sentence states, 'When centred upon residential areas, street prostitution and kerb-crawling can significantly reduce the quality of life enjoyed by a local population.'

Because the idea of 'significance' has numerical and statistical connotations, you should expect any document that claims to be fact-based to back it up with numbers. Did this paper do so? No.

The paper states 'tackling kerb-crawling and street prostitution in an area leads to its displacement or deflection to alternative sites.' It added, 'although there was some evidence of displacement, it was to areas such as the nearby shopping streets, which residents found less objectionable.'

House prices and the appearance of propriety was what mattered, not sex workers' safety and health. The only result desired – and obtained – was that the streetwalkers moved to a less populated area. It is a result that puts them at higher risk of attack.

Contrary to popular belief, streetwalkers don't just jump into any car. In fact, streetwalkers often pool strategies for reducing harm. They share number plates and descriptions of dodgy kerb crawlers, vet clients and only go to places they know. Outreach services like drop-in centres and night vans keep 'ugly mugs' books and are valuable point of contact. Programmes such as National Ugly Mugs provide a way for sex workers who don't want to go to the police to put out warnings about dangerous attackers. Sex workers perform a balancing act between maximising client exposure, while avoiding potential harm. The harm reduction approach is not perfect, but it fulfils a need, and is better than the alternatives.

Balsall Heath in Birmingham, where prostitutes once sat in the windows of flats along Cheddar Road, started to be targeted in the 1990s by vigilantes. Groups of men went after the women, both while they were working and when they weren't. It was a campaign of flat out harassment.

Harassment forces sex workers to get into clients' cars quickly, and be unable to avoid dangerous kerb crawlers. When vigilantes and police roam the pavements, sex workers wait until the wee hours to come out, making them more isolated and vulnerable to harm[liii].

Prostitutes left Balsall Heath alright, but not for different of work. They simply relocated, many going two miles away to Edgbaston, and the cycle began anew.

Displacement can also mean going from streetwalking to other ways of making money. High-profile crackdown results in arrests, which translate to fines that sex workers, burdened with criminal records, may unable to pay except by more prostitution or by fraud, shoplifting, and dealing drugs.[liv]

In the Scottish port city of Aberdeen, a tolerance zone for sex workers around the harbour was introduced in 2001. That ended with passage of the Prostitution (Public Places) (Scotland) Act in 2007. In the following months the city centre experienced a statistical increase in petty crimes.

Quay Services, which operates a drop-in centre, reported that sex workers became more afraid to seek assistance, and the number of women coming to the centre dropped to 'just a handful.'[lv] There was evidence that displacing sex workers led to more activity in the sex trade, not less – convictions for solicitation tripled.[lvi] This kind of 'crime shuffling' takes prostitution out of one area and puts it on another. It only resembles an improvement if you fail to look at the full picture.

High reoffending rates are inevitable when people are seen as only criminals, no matter what they do next. It is difficult to function in the straight world with a record. Many bosses are reluctant to hire someone with a criminal past. In some US states, being convicted of soliciting sex puts you on the sex offenders' register as well. Illinois, for instance, lists 'Public indecency' and 'Indecent solicitation of an adult' as worthy of sex offender status.

The opponents of sex work endorse policies that make a person's life outcomes narrower, harder, and more punishing. The Poppy Project for example, in its response to the Home Office's Paying the Price consultation on prostitution, reiterated that its agenda was to continue criminalize sex work. Slogans about rescue and 'turning lives around' are a red herring when no one will give you a job. The spiral of hopelessness is not broken by pat answers and 'tough on crime' posturing.

This also a knock-on effect on how sex workers are viewed by the public. If someone who has ever done sex work is murdered, her death is reported in the media not as 'woman killed,' but as 'prostitute killed.' Fiction, news, and ideology all spend a lot of time emphasising that it's usual, and even acceptable, to think of these people as inherently bad.

'The Yorkshire Ripper' Peter Sutcliffe escaped detection by police until he finally killed a woman who wasn't a sex worker. It happens over and over. Jill Meagher, killed in Sydney, Australia, was attacked while walking home by a man who was already known to have committed sexual offences against sex workers. Until a non-sex worker dies, no one cares, or pursues investigation with the vigour the crimes deserve.

Sex workers are targeted because of the message society sends about their lives having no value. Gary Ridgway, the Green River Killer, murdered forty-eight women in America in the early 1980s. He said: 'I picked prostitutes as victims because they were easy to pick up without being noticed. I knew they would not be reported missing right away and might never be reported missing. I thought I could kill as many of them as I wanted without getting caught.' It wasn't the commercial sex angle that was attractive to him, but knowing no one would care.

There are some working for positive change: in Liverpool, England, the Merseyside police have in the last decade taken a human rights approach to sex work. Instead of seeing workers as criminals, they approach crimes against sex workers as hate crimes. This has opened up a level of trust that rarely exists elsewhere. Assistant Chief Constable Chris Armitt states "The Merseyside model aims to build trust and confidence amongst sex workers to report when they are attacked, which allows the police to identify and arrest dangerous people who pose a threat to the whole of society."

National Ugly Mugs, a UK-based charity, offers support through technology. Their phone app helps sex workers share information about violent offenders directly and without involving police if they do not feel safe doing so. Alex Feis-Bryce, founder and former CEO of NUM, states: "Almost half of sex workers who receive our alerts have avoided a dangerous offender as a result. The warnings work; the challenge is getting them to as many sex workers as possible."

But the message sent by recent laws is only making that job harder. In Ireland, where Swedish-style laws were recently passed criminalizing parts of sex work, attacks against sex workers are on the rise. Ugly Mugs IE received 1,635 reports from sex workers who were concerned about clients in the five months since the law change, a 61 per cent increase on the same period last year. 137 of the incidents involved violence, including sexual assault.[lvii] Would-be attackers are hearing that the police and lawmakers don't care about sex workers loud and clear.

The Wild West may loom large in our imaginations, but in reality it did not last long at all. In the years following the US Civil War, the federal government started preparing western territories to become fully fledged states. Lawmaking procedures and regional government were standardized. As well as bringing in a considerable amount of red tape, this also helped pave the way for a population boom.

Increased migration brought a greater prudishness to the West. As churches began to overtake saloons, new arrivals were shocked by toleration of prostitution. In 1890 an alliance pressured the US Congress to form a national crime commission to investigate the sex trade. When Congress refused, the busybodies started their own.

The reports produced by these 'vice committees' were cited in forty-three cities' bans on the sex trade. They claimed to be objective, yet contained material that was strong-armed from sex workers and used to blackmail political opponents. Social purity movements forced 'soiled doves' into workhouses to 'rehabilitate' them. Young women deemed to be at risk were forcibly removed from their homes. With a combination of dodgy methods and underhand tactics, opponents of prostitution transformed their morality crusades into political power.

Reports that are written today are the intellectual heirs of these dishonest tactics, designed to sway government policy and force public opinion into line with their agendas.

Back in the nineteenth and early twentieth centuries, eugenicists believed that inherited degeneracy and 'feeble-mindedness' caused women to enter prostitution. Today, the party line is that prostitutes were sexually abused as children, and are emotionally unstable, or otherwise incapable of making their own decisions. We can't speak for ourselves. Therefore it is up to what Laura Agustin called the 'rescue industry' to step in.

The work of Melissa Farley is typical of this genre of fiction. Farley directs the Prostitution Research and Education organization in San Francisco. Farley self-publishes her research, bypassing academic peer review, then broadcasts the results through an network she founded herself.

In 'Prostitution and Trafficking in Nevada: Making the connections,' Farley claimed 90 per cent of sex workers 'wish they could get out.' But prostitution in Nevada is illegal, except for the highly-regulated 'pussy penitentiary' brothels in rural counties where the women are compelled to work long shifts and multiple weeks without days off, and where they are forbidden even to bring their own cars to the compounds. So the only people she interviewed were by definition either working illegally, or confined to bunker-like workplaces far from home. It is not representative of sex work in general, and does not include control groups of other sex workers anywhere.

Is job dissatisfaction confined to sex work? Across all employment sectors, less than 40 per cent of under-25s are satisfied with their work.[lviii] Even respectable jobs like teaching have problems, with 40 per cent of qualified UK teachers leaving due to stress and unhappiness within two years[lix]. Job dissatisfaction is not unique to sex work, and a projected 10 per cent satisfaction rate (in other words, 90 per cent of employees wishing they could get out) in unskilled work is common. Though, of course, there actually are studies showing far higher rates of job satisfaction in sex workers to contrast with the grim picture engineered in her study. Farley doesn't mention any of them.

One of Farley's other papers, reporting on post-traumatic stress disorder, recruited respondents at drug abuse drop-in centres, collecting data one would expect to have higher rates of mental trauma than even other sex workers. Again, there was no control population[lx]. Studies of PTSD in sex workers have been heavily criticised for being carried out by people who do not have the appropriate qualifications.[lxi]

The criticism has gained momentum. In September 2011, Dr Calum Bennachie filed a complaint with the American Psychology Association asking that they rescind the membership of Melissa Farley.

In the complaint, Dr Bennachie lists a number of reasons for doing so.[lxii] The reasons include factual errors in her papers, a failure to seek required ethical approval, and more. Bennachie also notes that 'she claimed to be able to diagnose sex workers as having post-traumatic stress disorder, despite using a flawed questionnaire, and not doing in depth interviews.' Such practices would clearly breach sections 5.01 and 8.10 of the APA's Code of Ethics.

Many self-described second wave feminists like Farley continue their campaigns with little or no supporting data. For instance, radical feminist Julie Bindel wrote in 2010 'prostitution is both the cause and consequence of inequality between men and women,'[lxiii] a logical impossibility if ever there was one.

Sex work laws worldwide vary widely, with different outcomes. The decriminalization of prostitution in New Zealand is one example. In general the vast majority of sex workers, whether streetwalkers or call girls, would prefer decriminalization over their jobs being illegal. But until this ground-breaking societal experiment was undertaken, no one really had data that could show definitively what the effect would be.

In 2003, New Zealand opted to overturn their laws that criminalized prostitution. The people most visibly affected by the law were streetwalkers in larger cities like Auckland, where in 2003 about 360 girls were estimated by police to be working. Streetwalkers represent about 11 per cent of the total number of prostitutes in the country.[lxiv]

Suddenly the world's focus was on New Zealand: would this change the sex trade there, and if so, how? Would it benefit the women, or harm them? What would it do to neighborhoods, to tourism, to the country's international image?

An evaluation released several years later showed that the number of sex workers changed very little – and in some places, the numbers of them on the streets actually decreased – compared to before sex work was legal. In Auckland, the estimated number of girls working the streets decreased significantly, from 360 to 106. People working in massage parlors and other establishments expressed a desire to stay in the work because of the financial rewards.[lxv]

In 2010, interviews with over 700 sex workers in New Zealand were published.[lxvi] The number of interviews represents 12 per cent of the estimated 5932 prostitutes in the country, a far higher national survey than in any study of sex workers ever conducted. It concluded that the majority entered and stayed in the sex trade for financial reasons, that they felt the new laws gave them more protection, and that the result was positive changes for safety and health.

Many reported social stigma was still a problem, but that they had become more willing (and able) to report crimes to the police. Which surely represents a victory for women's safety. Indeed, since then, being a sex worker in New Zealand has been rated safer than being an ambulance nurse.

How does New Zealand's decriminalization model compare to other countries? On the other side of the world, in Sweden, a law was passed in 1999 – sexköpslagen – that criminalized the buyers (but not the providers) of sex. Norway and Iceland adopted similar laws in 2009. France and Northern Ireland followed suit in 2016.

In July 2010 the Swedish government attempted for the first time to evaluate how the law change had gone. They only had official data about street prostitution, as other sex activities have become harder to identify as a result of sexköpslagen. It also included data from only seven active sex workers and seven former sex workers, a small sample by any standard. The evaluation compared the same time period to streetwalking activity in Denmark, where there was no such law. Those data came from a Copenhagen NGO whose numbers claimed the number of streetwalkers in Denmark was six times higher than it actually is.[lxvii]

Reports commissioned by others paint a very grim picture of the reality on Sweden now. Amnesty International confirms that sex workers have been denied medical care when they report sexual assault, with evicting them from their homes a priority instead, even when they have serious injuries.

In France it took less than a year for the negative effects to be felt. Trans sex workers in particular found themselves having to work in more and more isolated conditions, with violence against them spiraling out of control – and police more concerned with who their clients were than who their attackers were.[lxviii]

In Sweden, the country's largest human trafficking convictions came after the law was passed. In Iceland, which implemented similar laws, trafficking has skyrocketed, a result to be expected whenever a black market is created.[lxix] The sex workers will still exist, but now they turn to traffickers and criminals to protect them instead of law enforcement. They have no other choice.

So why is it popular, if the results are difficult to track and point towards causing harm? Not because of the evidence – but because it fits a preferred ideology in which sex workers and their clients *must be punished.*

The strict laws of the Swedish model that make clients into criminals also affect people living with sex workers – and even sex workers' families. There are already cases in which sex workers' children have been charged with pimping because they were living with a sex worker and not paying rent.

A large recent survey of sex workers in the UK showed 81.5% felt they would be less safe if the "Swedish model" of client criminalization was brought in. 83% of support organizations agreed. When asked what legislative model they preferred, over 60% of organizations and 70% of sex workers felt full decriminlization would keep them safer. In all the results, only 3% of organizations and 2% of sex workers wanted the Swedish model.[lxx]

Hold on a moment – if only 3% of outreach organizations support the Swedish model, why are there so many groups apparently pushing for it? Because those groups that do, and the people in them, are not frontline outreach. They are not the ones staffing drop-in centres, sitting in vans, handing out condoms and coffee to women on the streets on a winter's night. They are fronts for ideology-based lobbying efforts and never come into contact with the people whose livelihoods they are trying to take away.

Why do people with real experience reject the Swedish model? Because it leads to harm and abuse. Here is one unfortunate example. In 2013 a Swedish sex work activist, Petite Jasmine, was murdered by her ex-husband. Because the government knew she was an escort, they took her two children away and awarded custody to her ex, ignoring his history violent abuse. It was during a state-supervised visit, the first in many months, that her ex attacked and killed her in front of their kids.

For the 'crime' of being a sex worker, the government gave children to a murderous abuser. Those kids will now grow up without both parents and scarred irreparably by what they have seen.

Meanwhile in Canada, laws – and attitudes – nearly changed. Terri-Jean Bedford a dominatrix whose brothel the Bondage Bungalow had been subjected to numerous Canadian police raids, court cases, and appeals, put her case to the courts from the early 1990s. After two decades defending her right to a livelihood, Bedford's argument found favor with Ontario Superior Court Justice Susan Himel. Himel's judgment ruled that prostitutes' rights to 'life, liberty and security' under the Canadian Charter of Rights and Freedoms were being violated by aggressive policing.

The ruling challenged three laws restricting those activities – keeping a brothel, communicating for the purposes of prostitution, and living off the proceeds of prostitution. In a 132-page ruling, the judge said: 'I find that the danger faced by prostitutes greatly outweighs any harm which may be faced by the public.'[lxxi]

The government side argued that all forms of prostitution are unsafe, and making brothels legal would only attract sex tourists and human traffickers to Canada. Himel rejected those opinions, stating they were 'issues that are, in my view, incidental to the case ....' She criticized Melissa Farley's evidence, saying 'some experts made bold assertions without properly outlined bases for their claims and were unwilling to qualify their opinions in the face of new facts provided.'

It was appealed, however, and the case went all the way to Canada's Supreme Court. The Court agreed broadly with Himel and the earlier judgment and suspended the existing criminal codes around prostitution. The government was forced to come up with a response. Many had hoped this would lead to full decriminalization, such as New Zealand has.

Unfortunately the Canadian government implemented the Swedish model: the set of laws that criminalizes vulnerable people's income, turns sex workers into unwilling sources of evidence, harms families and, ultimately, encourages rather than discourages trafficking. The same laws that led to Jasmine's murder. The success Terri Jean Bedford fought so hard to achieve was wiped out by dogmatic feminist propaganda with proven harmful outcomes.

A lot of people new to sex workers' rights often call for "legalizing and taxing it." Famously, the Netherlands has legalized prostitution, as do some other places – brothels in Germany and in Nevada are also examples of legalization.

But legalization is not ideal for many reasons. And anyway, sex workers already pay taxes... I know I did! Why don't sex workers support legalization?

Legalization differs from full decriminalization in that it only permits sex work in licensed premises. This could mean sex workers have to appear on public registers using their real names, and have intrusive medical histories taken. In Germany, public records of where registered sex workers' names and addresses have been used as a tool of harassment and intimidation. In Nevada, it means workers can find themselves locked in the brothels, with laws preventing them from going out locally. It also creates a two-tier system where people able to 'clock in' for shifts are permitted, but people with chaotic lives still find themselves having to rely on a black market to earn money.

Here's an analogy: as a freelance writer, I can go to work for any employer in their premises, but I can also work for myself. My work is decriminalized. I choose the conditions of my labor while at the same time still being responsible for declaring my income and paying taxes. Is it freedom if writing is only permitted provided you work for certain newspapers? Of course not.

A system of legalization instead of decriminalization affects the most disadvantaged. It can also, strangely enough, affect the upper end of sex work. In 2015 my good friend Conchita van der Waal, a woman who worked in banking by day and was a fetish companion by night, was fired from her job at the Dutch National Bank when her extracurricular activities were discovered. Even though her work contract did not forbid any kind of second career, and even though the widespread impression people have is of "tolerant" Holland, she was denied access to her pension, harassed by Amsterdam city officials who accused her of running an illegal brothel, and feared her children might be taken out of her and her husband's care.

Under a system of decriminalization, this would not have happened. Instead of licensed legal and illegal sex workers, decriminalization would allow someone to work both in legal establishments like Holland's licensed kamers and privathuisen, or freelance on the side like an independent escort. As with all other types of freelance work, the responsibility to declare income and pay tax, and to look after one's health would be in the hands of the individual.

Despite occasional setbacks like in Canada, the sex worker rights movement continues to grow. Groups like the Asia Pacific Network of Sex Workers (APNSW), and the Desiree Alliance in the US, are made up of sex workers who have much to say about the policies affecting them. Sex workers have started to appear in debates, on television and radio, and even in cover stories for the New York Times Magazine discussing their fight for rights.

The data supporting decriminalization is also gathering. In 2015, Amnesty International, after a worldwide consultation looking at all available data, endorsed supporting decrim. They ignored the pleadings of Hollywood elites like Meryl Streep and Kate Winslet, and instead listened to sex workers and researchers. The Home Affairs Select

Committee on Prostitution in the UK came to similar conclusions. The rational arguments for why harm reduction and decriminalization provide better outcomes than punitive laws are winning out.

Amnesty was the latest in a trend for high-profile organizations to back decriminalization. UNAids supports it as a harm reduction strategy that helps to stem the spread of HIV. UN Women backs it too. The World Health Organization (WHO) supports decriminalization. So too does the ACLU, although it has been reluctant to publicly support incarcerated sex workers – perhaps the fact so many other respectable groups now back decrim will change that. In the UK, the Liberal Democrat and Green parties have official policy supporting sex work decriminalization.

How does it make sense to attack particular kinds of physical work, when people make money from their bodies in other ways? Surely, by that logic, fashion modelling and ballet dancing ought to be banned as well. Men's bodies are exploited by war – few dare endorse putting the Army out of business. There are vulnerable and exploited people in all kinds of work, not just sex work. It makes more sense to attack the conditions that make them vulnerable, not the work they use to survive. Sex workers need more rights, not less power.

There is a lot of talk in politics about the need for 'evidence-based policy.' Sex workers – like Michaela Hague, like Petite Jasmine – have suffered the consequences of prejudice that leads to bad policy. The prohibition approach has not worked. It will never work.

Moral disapproval is a bad basis for policy making. The condescension heaped on people who do sex work is embarrassingly transparent. All this mealy-mouthed, 'Oh, but we want to help them, really.' By saddling people with criminal records and taking away their children?

As well as the happy, well-paid call girls there are unhappy, poor sex workers in need of support. Society should protect the unwilling and underage from exploitation as well as support workers demanding access to labor rights. The existence of abuses in some employment does not mean workers should be criminalized – the existence of a sweat shops doesn't make putting all clothing manufacturers out of business a good idea. It's time we saw that sex work is real work, too.

CHAPTER 4

Did You Know...

- *The numbers widely quoted about trafficking are incorrect*
- *Trafficking is more common in agriculture and domestic service than in the sex industry*
- *Many notable anti-trafficking charities have been proven frauds*
- *Most laws against sex trafficking criminalize the people they're meant to help*

In the years after the Berlin Wall fell, Eastern European gangs set up operations to smuggle profitable items like drugs, guns, and cigarettes. And, reportedly, women. As the story goes, they scooped up young women from their hometowns in the Eastern Bloc south to Greece. Once successfully inside Greece, the women could be transported within the EU without being stopped at the borders.

As stories of sex trafficking in mainland Europe grew more common, people became concerned about Eastern European women arriving in the West. Were they economic migrants, working unskilled jobs for ready cash? Or was it a more sinister trend, women being controlled by gangs of thugs?

In the absence of any figures people assumed the worst in all cases. The conventional wisdom was that the women were being trafficked. Government agencies, police forces, and charities joined forces – and obtained funding – to deal with what they claimed was a widespread criminal trend. Numbers started to circulate as if they were fact.

The closer we look at the truth about trafficking, the more we find not women and children being saved from terrible fates, but powerful agencies claiming money and attention for themselves while the people they supposedly rescue are arrested, deported, and fall through society's cracks.

Open any newspaper or magazine, and the story is the same. 'Sex

Slave in Suburbia,' in Glamour magazine, claimed there are half a million women trafficked in the EU for sex. Is the number even plausible? As far as figures go, it's absurdly high. No source for the number is offered.

The article goes on to claim that punters are 'more likely' to visit a trafficked sex worker than a non-trafficked one, though police records do not back this up. Where is all the misinformation coming from?

The problem starts with a deceptively simple question: how many trafficked sex workers are there? It's an easy question to ask, but almost impossible to answer. That hasn't stopped people who have claimed to know the answer from claiming unrealistic totals though.

This is the story of how a speculative number tentatively suggested by researchers became a vastly inflated 'truth.' It involves media and government misinformation, with each iteration of the story straying further and further from reality. And, ironically, putting at risk the very lives they intend to save.

When nineteen Chinese seafood workers drowned in an English bay in 2004, it highlighted the appalling conditions forced workers live in. They were packed into flats together, sleeping four to a mattress n the floor, transported to and from long hours of work in the back of vans. With no English language skills or local contacts they did not have local knowledge and could not respond to warnings that the tide was coming in faster than they could outrun it. Of the 14 survivors, nine were registered as asylum seekers and five were completely unknown to immigration services.

The majority of confirmed trafficking cases are, like the Chinese workers in Morecambe Bay, unrelated to sex work. Media coverage equates all trafficking with sex trafficking, but most trafficked people are brought in for domestic labour, agriculture, and food processing. As the crises that drive refugees out of places like Libya and Syria worsen, there is also a large amount of non-work related trafficking solely to get people across borders so they won't be turned back when claiming asylum.

Not all trafficking is sex trafficking of women. Of national referrals made in the UK in 2009, 74% were female, 26% were male. Sexual exploitation accounts for 43% of victims; the rest are trafficked for manual and domestic labor. In 2016, the Crown Prosecution Service noted the proportion of trafficked men had risen to 40% (but still reported these incidents as 'violence against women and girls' anyway). When they break down trafficking categories by age, all children are assumed to be female.

Worldwide, the United Nation's International Labor Organization

(ILO) estimates that no more than 21 per cent of trafficked people are in forced sexual labour. The majority instead end up in jobs other people don't want, or are taken on by employers paying under the minimum wage. Vietnamese and Chinese children have been found working on UK cannabis farms, for example. The needs of trafficked men are rarely, if ever, addressed in discussion and policy[lxxii].

To listen to the media, though, you wouldn't imagine trafficking comes in flavours other than sex.

Why is it so important to get the numbers right? Several reasons. First, there is competition over government grants for groups that assist victims. Until recently most of this money went to groups such as the Poppy Project, which only serves female victims, and only in London. So if trafficking affects men as well, and occurs in places like Morecambe Bay, there would be good reason to question whether giving money to groups with such a narrow focus is a good idea.

Another reason is that it's hard to generate publicity for a problem if it's experienced by people no one cares about. People who are poor and from overseas are perceived to be the cause of job losses. With the majority of trafficked people working in domestic and agricultural labor, they are beneath contempt in the eyes of many. No one cares about their welfare. But women and – especially – children? Potentially being used for sex? Suddenly, you have a demographic people care about. Suddenly you have the makings of a moral panic.

In 2009 British MP Denis MacShane wrote a letter to the Guardian claiming 18,000 young women were trafficked into Britain 'as sex slaves.' Later he told Parliament that the number was in fact 25,000. The source for these numbers was reportedly a Home Office document[lxxiii].

The then Solicitor General, Vera Baird, challenged MacShane and his source, the Daily Mirror. She claimed that the real number of women was closer to 4000.

It turns out even this was an exaggeration. The number, which is difficult to estimate, was nevertheless expanded beyond all credibility.

How would you start estimating the size of such a problem, when it is hard to detect victims? Making estimates with limited information is called a 'Fermi problem.' Enrico Fermi, one of the physicists who worked on the Manhattan Project, was reputedly able to make accurate guesses at numbers others considered unknowable. The classic example was his estimate of how many piano tuners there are in Chicago. He was able to come up with an answer – 150 – that if not exact, was within a reasonable error margin.

Here's an example of a Fermi problem in action. I was at pub quiz one week, and our team was tied for the lead. The tiebreaker was the question 'How many performances did Yul Brynner have as the King of Siam in The King and I on Broadway?' As the only former drama geek in our team, it came down to me. I calculated that Brynner probably did eight performances a week (once a day and twice on Sundays, as the saying goes). It's a full-time job, so minus a two-week holiday, Brynner was probably performing fifty weeks a year. I wasn't sure how many years the show ran for but knew he had been in at least one revival of the popular musical, so let's say ten years of being the king in total. That makes an estimate of:

8 shows a week x 50 weeks a year x 10 years = 4000 shows

Sounds pretty high, right? The other team probably thought so too, because they guessed 300. We won the tiebreak (and the quiz) because, as it turned out, the real answer is 4525. Picking a number out of thin air, as the other team did, is fraught with error. It's hard to make good guesses with no information. Apply some basic knowledge and your accuracy goes up rapidly.

Fermi problems are great for pub quizzes, but common-or-garden wild guesses are not always the stuff on which good research is built. At the very least, estimating a number should fulfil two major criteria:

1. The assumptions must have some foundation in reality. In the Yul Brynner example, eight Broadway performances a week is reasonable; eighty wouldn't be.
2. The method of calculation needs to be explained. The other person on my team would have been sceptical of 4000 if they hadn't seen my reasoning.

Data from the UK Network of Sex Work Projects (UKNSWP) in 2009 estimates a total of about 50,000 sex workers in the UK.[lxxiv] The 1999 estimate by Hilary Kinnell for the European Network for HIV/STD Prevention in Prostitution (EUROPAP) project, of 80,000, is more commonly cited. [lxxv] If the trafficking hype was real, that would mean anywhere from one in twelve to one in two sex workers was the victim of trafficking. The numbers of sex slaves quoted by Denis MacShane are so unrealistic that, if true, they would account for the majority of prostitution in Britain. Regardless of how you feel about sex work, there are self-evidently many non-immigrants in it who (since they haven't crossed borders) can't possibly have been trafficked. The majority of street-based prostitutes in the UK are British, and almost all the rest are

EU nationals who already have the right to live and work in Britain.

Researchers Liz Kelly and Linda Regan attempted to estimate a number in 1998 by surveying reports filed with police forces. The number they came up with was seventy-one. This included women who were trafficked against their will, but also women who willingly arrived – perhaps illegally – to the UK for sex work. In other words, Kelly and Regan's total included both willing and unwilling sex migrants.

If people who cross borders voluntarily can be called 'trafficked,' then what is 'trafficking,' exactly? The Palermo Protocol to Prevent, Suppress and Punish Trafficking in Persons Especially Women and Children, part of the 2000 UN Convention against Transnational Organized Crime defines 'trafficking' as:

> ... the threat or use of force or other forms of coercion, of abduction, of fraud, of deception, of the abuse of power or of a position of vulnerability or of the giving or receiving of payments or benefits to achieve the consent of a person having control over another person, for the purpose of exploitation.

In other words, illegal migration for purposes of economic advantage, if undertaken willingly and fully informed, is not trafficking.[lxxvi]

But let's assume every single one of those seventy-one women was brought to the UK unwillingly. Kelly and Regan then grapple with under-reporting. Without any hard information, they guessed an equal number might have been missed by the police and doubled the seventy-one – so, a total of 142 women. That's the lower boundary of their estimate.

For the upper boundary, they guessed that trafficking might be undetected by a factor of as much as twenty times. So, the upper boundary of the estimate was 1420. The absolute maximum which, they emphasised, was speculative.

To summarise: the estimate for the absolute highest number of trafficked women in the UK for the year of 1998 was 1420. (No credible estimate methodology has emerged since.) What does this tell us? That sex trafficking is possibly underreported, and no one knows the numbers.

That highest possible estimate of 1420 is considerably smaller – only about a third – of the number Vera Baird used. It is smaller than the claims made by MacShane by a factor of seventeen. How did that happen?

At first, the paper was cited with only a small error in reporting the results. Then the Salvation Army and Churches Alert to Sex Trafficking Across Europe (CHASTE) reported not Regan and Kelly's range of values, but the estimated maximum value as if it were the number of actual reports. They updated the year as well – 'An estimated 1,420 women were trafficked into the UK in 2000 for the purposes of constrained prostitution.' This is entirely a lie.

In 2003 the Home Office took inaccurate estimates a step further. Assuming all foreign-born women in Soho walkups to be trafficked, plus 75 per cent of foreign sex workers throughout the UK, plus 10 per cent foreign call girls gave the total of 3812 women in forced sex work in Britain. Yes, this included even EU citizens who could travel and work there freely.

That number, rounded up to 4000 for no reason, is widely quoted without acknowledging that it is an inflation of someone else's highest possible number.

In 2006 the Commons Joint Committee on Human Rights heard this number entered into the Hansard as if it were a fact. Interested parties now had the handy 'government figures showing' 4000 women being trafficked without the hassle of having to question whether that was true. Radical feminist Julie Bindel, perhaps best known for her statements that all men should be locked in prison camps, claimed '[s]tudies have found that at least 70 per cent of women working in UK brothels are trafficked from places such as Africa, Asia and Eastern Europe.' This had to be retracted later by the newspaper as no such study exists.[lxxvii]

The number 4000 also appeared in a US Department of State document on worldwide trafficking (although interestingly as a number representing all trafficking, not just sex trafficking)[lxxviii]. The Christian charity Care picked up on it as well, and the Salvation Army replied by asserting the number was now at least 4000.

From there to 25,000 is actually only a matter of multiplying it by six and a bit, in spite of the fact that the estimate used as the origin for all of these dodgy calculations was itself already an overcount.

When challenged to justify his number of 25,000 per year on Newsnight, Dennis MacShane had no firm sources to hand[lxxix]. He said he read it in the Daily Mirror and that it came from the Home Office, but the Mirror and HO documents do not contain that claim[lxxx]. MacShane was forced to admit he did not know anything about the numbers he was using.

Nick Davies, who reported on the phenomenon, commented, '… the cycle has been driven by political opportunists and interest groups in pursuit of an agenda … an unlikely union of evangelical Christians with feminist campaigners, who pursued the trafficking tale to secure their greater goal, not of regime change, but of legal change to abolish all prostitution.'[lxxxi]

In the US, human trafficking has been a hot topic for years. But the numbers, like Britain and the EU's, are less impressive than the headlines would have you believe. The US Department of Justice's special report "Characteristics of Suspected Human Trafficking Incidents, 2007-08," revealed only 1 in 10 reported incidents contained any trafficking features at all (and most of those did not lead to convictions). While statistics of proven trafficking cases worldwide show labor trafficking to be the more serious problem, sex trafficking still accounted for 10 times as many investigations.

In the Netherlands, a 2016 estimate by the Dutch National Rapporteur on Human Trafficking was that 1.5 per cent of sex workers in Amsterdam are trafficked, which is considerably lower than the numbers thrown around by others like Bindel that start at an astounding – and statistically indefensible – 70 per cent! In Cambodia, believed by all to have the worst sex trafficking problem in the world, the percentage of forcibly trafficked sex workers that can be confirmed is about 5 per cent. That is the highest. Anything greater than that anywhere else in the world will have been produced by stretching the definitions, overcounting, and guesswork. And discounting the lived experiences of real sex workers. Very high numbers typically include foreign born women who are in sex work by choice.

Rarely, if ever, is the definition of trafficking explained in the media. This violates the second principle of the realistic estimate: show your work clearly. It's the kind of sloppy calculation that throws all conclusions into question. It's bad Fermi.

Grahame Maxwell, chief constable for North Yorkshire, put the hype about sex-specific trafficking into perspective. 'There are more people trafficked for labour exploitation than there are for sexual exploitation. We need to redress the balance here. People just seem to grab figures from the air.' [lxxxii]

In 2007, police forces across the UK started a wide-scale investigation into sex trafficking. Called Pentameter Two, with the co-operation of all fifty-five police forces in England, Wales, Scotland, and Northern Ireland, the Border Agency and the Crown Prosecution Service, you would expect the result to be nothing short of comprehensive.

This operation used every method at police disposal, including brothel raids, undercover operations, and co-ordinated information, was not successful. As Nick Davies detailed in a series of articles for the Guardian, Pentameter Two resulted in five convictions of men accused of importing women and forcing them to work as prostitutes. Five convictions across the entire country.[lxxxiii] And, it was later revealed, none of those were detected by actions in the Pentameter Two effort, but due to other investigations.

Did it save anyone? During Pentameter Two in 2008 and Pentameter One in 2006, over 1300 locations were raided. A total of 255 women were 'rescued.' That suggests that the proportion of forced women in sex work is far lower than the 80 per cent claimed by Fiona Mactaggart MP. (Who, it turns out, was using as her source of information a survey of street-based sex workers. In San Francisco. From 1982.[lxxxiv])

Were they trafficked? Impossible to say since by late 2009, police had lost track of most of them.[lxxxv] Of the 255 women, sixteen were deported, thirty-six of them returned home and thirty-seven accepted victim support services. The whereabouts of the rest – 166 women – are unknown.

It seems that the 255 women, rather than being the victims of trafficking, were voluntary migrants. Dr Belinda Brooks-Gordon at Birkbeck College who specializes in sexuality and the law, commented 'We do know a lot of women in the former Russian states who are working in sex industry and who are desperate to come here. They want to earn more money here – they are migrant workers like any other workers.'

In Northern Ireland, the numbers again turn out to be smaller than expected. With twenty-five cases of human trafficking in 2009/2010, seventeen of which involved sexual exploitation – the number of trafficking victims is less than one per 100,000 people.[lxxxvi]

Still, even if only a small number of sex traffickers are operating in this country, that should be cause for worry, and who could disagree? In theory, yes. If police funding and time were unlimited, every crime should be investigated to the utmost.

Pentameter Two and other such operations are not cases of unlimited money, or of people, or of time. Police forces were made to take part but no additional money and staff were provided. Funding is allocated under the Reflex project, which receives £20 million a year, but with no specific provision for Pentameter Two.[lxxxvii] Police were required to conduct undercover investigations and raids – in addition to whatever trafficking-detection activities they already carried out – without any extra support. This diversion of resources resulted in not one fresh conviction.

Let's go back to Denis MacShane's estimate of 25,000 trafficked sex slaves. That story claimed women were forced to have sex with thirty men a day. If true, that means 750,000 men exploit sex slaves every day. That's huge.

'How is it that three quarters of a million men can find a sex slave every day but when highly trained police officers run a special nationwide operation lasting months they can only find at best a couple of hundred women that they think might be victims of trafficking?' asked Professor Julia O'Connell Davidson on Radio 4[lxxxviii].

Project Acumen, set up by Britain's Association of Chief Police Officers (Acpo), released its findings in 2010. Titled Setting The Record, the report focuses on sex trafficking and where the people come from, as well as their circumstances.[lxxxix]

Based on this, the Telegraph reported 12,000 'confirmed' trafficked women were in the UK.[xc] It goes on: 'in a typical example, a woman smuggled into the UK does not know that she is going to be used as a prostitute, but is forced into selling her body to pay off a £30,000 "debt-bond".'

Does the report actually say this? It doesn't. Where does 12,000 come from? It's not clear.

Project Acumen's report didn't locate 12,000 women, much less interview anything like that many. It is based on interviews with 210 foreign and forty-four British sex workers located at 142 premises in England and Wales. Of the 210 migrants, none were kidnapped or held hostage. Only one was the victim of violence.

202 of the 210 knew they would be working as prostitutes in the UK. Of the other eight, it is unclear whether they were misled about location rather than the work. Two dozen were labeled trafficked – nineteen Asians and five Eastern Europeans. The criteria, however, were not determined by the UN's Palermo Protocol, but by a complex set of 'dimensions,' that again, do not seem to distinguish willing (if perhaps illegal) migration from unwilling trafficking.

The number 12,000 pops up in the report – an estimate of about 4000 trafficked sex slaves pulled out of thin air, with 8000 more from 'vulnerable' populations. No sources for these numbers exist. The paper qualifies its statements with 'most are likely to fall short of the trafficking threshold.' Or, in other words, there is no way to prove their claims either way. It continues:

Approximately 3,700 of them are from Asia; there may be significant cultural factors which prevent them from exiting prostitution or seeking help, but they tend to have day-to-day control over their activities and do not consider themselves to be debt-bonded. A further estimated 4,100 are from Eastern Europe; although many are legally entitled to live and work in the UK, they tend to speak little English and because they live and work in areas they are unfamiliar with they are overly reliant on their controllers. Most made a conscious decision to become involved in prostitution, albeit with limited alternatives, and the financial rewards on offer are considered to be a significant pull factor for these individuals.

Figures from the UK Human Trafficking Centre confirm the number of trafficked women is smaller than is reported. In the twelve-month period from April 2009 to March 2010, 709 referrals were made to the centre, with the majority detected by border control rather than police. Of the 709 in that year, just 319 were referred as suspected cases of sex trafficking. Only about half the cases had been processed by the time of the report, but of those, 68 per cent were dismissed as not trafficking.[xci]

Even Antislavery International has gone so far as to say, 'Evidence shows that current measures have not improved the rate of trafficking convictions in the UK, and in some cases they actively undermine prosecutions.'[xcii]

Others invoked fiction to explain shortfalls. 'The Wire,' wrote Catherine Bennett in the Observer, 'showed just how tricky it can be when, with the best of intentions, the authorities attempt to organise human squalor.'[xciii]

The Wire was a television series about criminals and police in Baltimore, Maryland. Pentameter 2 received explicit UK government support, was co-ordinated across police areas, and diverted large amounts of resources. Assuming that a fictional plucky little band of cops in a US-based drama is an insight into a coordinated police operation across Britain is an argument that is at best lazy and at worst laughable.

The US has a higher population than the UK, and vast land borders with other countries, which have been customarily exploited for drug running and illegal migration.

Portland, Oregon, is the state's largest city, lying about 150 miles south of Seattle, Washington. The quality of living is high: Portland is frequently named one of the US's best cities to live in for its easy accessibility, robust economy, and access to nature.

In 2010 and 2011, the city became an unexpected target of reports on sex trafficking. Dan Rather dubbed the city 'Pornland.' Others called it the 'epicentre for child prostitution' and a 'hotbed of sex trafficking.' Actors such as Daryl Hannah and politicians descended for the Northwest Conference Against Trafficking to discuss what should be done to get this problem under control.

In November 2010, Portland's mayor, Sam Adams, declared to the press that his city had become 'stained' as a centre of sex trafficking.

Portland police, he claimed, report an average of two cases of child sex trafficking every week.

The problem with the number? It isn't true.

According to Sergeant Mike Geiger of the Portland sex crimes unit, police don't track such statistics. 'I am not sure where that is coming from,' he said. 'That's an unreliable number.' [xciv] So how did Portland become the focus of a moral panic?

In February 2009, an FBI investigation in Portland found seven prostitutes under the age of eighteen. This caught the media's attention, and they claimed strip clubs and permissive attitudes led middle-class girls to be tricked into prostitution. Little or no consideration was given to the question of why homeless teenagers – the ones most likely to start exchanging sex for money – were on the streets in the first place, or what could have been done to prevent that.

Politicians claimed the area was 'particularly attractive to traffickers,' leading to a 'particularly high prevalence of sexual exploitation of children.' Meanwhile, commissioners allocated $7 million to fight the 'problem' and $900,000 for a Portland shelter. On the basis of a handful teens – and again, no consideration for the larger problem of homelessness – about $8 million will be allocated to fight this 'epidemic.'

Blatant number inflation is common. A 2016 claim from the Heart of Texas Human Trafficking Coalition is that "79,000 kids [are] currently being trafficked in Texas" – in other words, five times the US total of sexually exploited children. How is this possible? The simple answer is that it isn't. Not unless you start playing fast and loose with definitions, which is exactly what is going on.

One frequently cited claim is that 300,000 youths in the US, Canada, and Mexico are at risk of sexual exploitation. [xcv] The US Department of Justice cites this statistic, as do UNICEF, CNN, and the National Center for Missing & Exploited Children. However, over time, people have begun to cite the number 300,000 as an actual count of trafficked US-only children.

Being 'at risk' of exploitation does not mean that all, or even many, of those young people will be sexually exploited. Of those who are, there no reason to think all, or even most, will be trafficked for paid sex. For instance the report itself confirms 'nearly all of it [sexual exploitation] occurs in the privacy of the child's own home (84%) ... 96% of all confirmed child sexual abuse cases are perpetrated by persons known either to the child or to the child's family.' Children are far more likely to be abused at home, yet that seems to concern no one.

What do the authors consider a risk? The tally includes such categories as children of migrants - in spite of the questionable assumption that immigration is a risk factor for child sexual abuse.

The study counted the number of runaways under eighteen. The authors then came up with a percentage they believed to be at risk of sexual exploitation based on interviews with fewer than 300 teens. Unsurprisingly, other statistics from the same report, such as 'only about 10% of the [confirmed sexually exploited] children we encountered are trafficked internationally' are not often mentioned. In any case, extrapolating from such a small group to cover all young people over an entire continent is statistically problematic and not a good basis for a nationwide estimate.

US statistics back this up: in 2016, arrests for trafficking were virtually zero in 48 of the 50 states (Texas and Minnesota, who bucked that trend, made about 100 arrests each).[xcvi] Long-range police stats collected by activist Norma Jean Almodovar also show the trend for underage prostitution has been in steep decline since the early 1980s.[xcvii]

Meanwhile on Facebook, stories proliferate like the mother in California who claimed she saved her children from trafficking because she saw two men in IKEA. The post went viral, even though trafficking survivors say the misinformation spread by people like her hurts, rather than helps, real investigations.[xcviii] Child abduction is not exactly common: as Dr Marty Klein notes, "There are about 200 stranger kidnappings in the U.S. every year. Your kid is more likely to get killed by lightning." Most children who go missing are runaways or abducted by their own parents.

And the laws that are meant to protect them? Backfire, massively. A Kansas teen named Hope Zeferjohn was ordered by her abuser to message another teen and try to get her to run away from home. Hope was sentenced to six years in prison for child sex trafficking, in spite of being coerced and a minor herself at the time.[xcix]

The US Bureau of Justice reports that between 1st January, 2007, and 30th September, 2008 task forces reported investigating 1229 alleged incidents of human trafficking.[c] Sex trafficking accounted for 1018 (83 per cent) of the alleged incidents. Of these, 391 (38 per cent) involved allegations of child sex trafficking.

Less than 10 per cent of the reported incidents turned out to be human trafficking. Allegations of forced adult prostitution accounted for 63 per cent of the rejected investigations that were ultimately found not to involve trafficking at all.

Over twenty-one months, only 120 cases of human trafficking were confirmed. That's less than six per month for the entire country. If we scale the results by population, this makes rates of confirmed trafficking in Britain and the US very similar to each other. It also indicates trafficking is very rare in both countries.

Most of the US cases did not involve foreigners: 63 per cent of those 'rescued' were US citizens.[ci] Of that 120, it is unclear how many were women, if any were underage, or how much of the trafficking was for the purposes of sex. Remember, the number of people trafficked for labour far outnumber the number trafficked for sex.

The FBI gets a piece of the action too. "Operation Cross Country" contributed $22.7 million for task forces in 2015 and $15.8 million in 2016, in addition to whatever costs were incurred by local field offices. The result? In 2016, a grand total of two arrests of suspected traffickers of 16- and 17-year-olds. Not even a ring: two unrelated, individual cases dealing with only one victim each. In such cases even the victims are not "rescued," they are usually arrested and slapped with prostitution or loitering charges.[cii]

A 2016 report from the US Justice Department recorded 1,130 arrests of underage individuals for prostitution in 2009. If you think this is rescue, think again - young offenders get not just detention and court fees, but criminal records that can exclude them from being eligible for social services, as well as making difficult to rent homes, get jobs, and apply for loans. The "victims services" offered to them at the time of arrest, if any, amount to no more than missionary and faith-based programs, or referrals to shelters that won't accept young people with criminal backgrounds.

Even the government knows - or should know - this is no kind of help. A DoJ-funded report from 2014 looking at the supposed help offered by the Salvation Army and similar services notes, "The common thread was of young people engaged in sex trades as the least-bad solution to meeting fundamental needs ... [prostitution] was never the only problem in these young people's lives and often not the most critical problem." The report strongly urged law enforcement to stop arresting these young people.[ciii]

However – and this is the disturbing part – there is a good reason for police to seize on overstated and debunked stats, and for feminists and others pushing the trafficking panic to start courting law enforcement as their preferred allies. That reason? Money.

The prison system in the US, partly privatized and highly profitable, has exploded in previous decades due to mandatory minimum sentences in the War on Drugs. But the times are changing. As many people, and increasingly many US states, embrace legalization of marijuana and a harm reduction, healthcare-based approach to harder drugs, where will new bodies to fill private prisons come from?

It doesn't take a genius to see that sex work, now heightened to "trafficking," is one candidate to fill those cells. Groups that currently divert money away from frontline outreach programs (as I will show in the next chapter) can now earn even more by delivering "awareness" and "training" to militarized law enforcement. If they can hitch their wagon to border security debates at the same time ICE is being beefed up? All the better for their bottom line.

Raids and arrests do not address the needs of people who may be trafficked. There has been little focus on identifying what potential victims would find helpful, instead channelling people into post-prison re-education that amounts to training seamstresses for sweatshop work. A human-rights-based approach to trafficking would prioritise the needs of potential victims over criminalizing them and shuttling them into low-paid wage slavery. But is anyone paying attention once the raids are over?

CHAPTER 5

Did You Know...

- *A network of far-right interests fund misleading research and campaigns worldwide*
- *There are links between anti-trafficking campaigns and white supremacy, anti-LGBT efforts, and abuse of women in institutions*
- *The money allocated to anti-trafficking is almost always misspent*

'Vice trade a disease time bomb,' yelled one headline. 'Police send STD info to suspects in prostitution sting,' advised another. Even the sports pages were not immune, with 'Aids and HIV warning to South Africa World Cup fans' featured prominently on the BBC website . The World Cup warnings, in particular, were widespread in the run-up to the football tournament in 2010.

Are the headlines accurate? Are prostitutes spreading sexually transmitted infections? Many believe sex workers play the central role in the transmission of STIs to the general public. But a huge amount of research over the past twenty years counters this belief.

Studies consistently show high rates of condom use in sex work, and low risks of HIV and other STI for women sex workers. Cohort studies have shown a low incidence of HIV infection in sex workers in Europe (0.2 cases per 100 person years in the United Kingdom). Decriminalization reduces HIV epidemics, averting 33-46% of infections in some countries.[civ]

Despite an increase in the rate of STIs in the general population, sex workers have shown a decline in infections. In the Netherlands, where prostitution is legal and workers' health monitored, sex workers have a lower rate of sexually transmitted infections than swingers.

The real vectors are not sex workers, most of whom use condoms, and are tested regularly for infections. In the UK, the population that is really experiencing a surge in STIs is the over-fifties. About 13,000 older men and women were diagnosed with STIs in 2009, double the number diagnosed in 2000 . Rather than prostitutes spreading disease, the real vectors seem to be people who assume that their partners are 'safe,' or people who were perhaps in committed relationships and marriages the last time public health campaigns about safer sex were saturating the media, but aren't monogamous anymore.

Still the headlines continued. 'Prostitutes flock to South Africa ahead of World Cup 2010.' claimed the Christian Science Monitor, with similar warnings in the Washington Post, New York Times, and virtually every English-language international paper. According to reports seeded by social work groups and charities, some 40,000 prostitutes were set to arrive in South Africa – coincidentally, the identical number that had been predicted (but never materialized) for Germany's World Cup in 2006.

Leaked diplomatic cables discuss the sex trafficking scare around that earlier World Cup. 'Over 20 NGOs throughout Germany have received government funds to conduct dozens of trafficking prevention and awareness campaigns.' The same cable discusses raids on Munich brothels in search of said trafficking victims, noting it couldn't find any. Another cable discusses raids, involving hundreds of police officers, in which seventy-four women were detained. '[P]olice findings demonstrate there has been no substantial increase in [trafficking in persons] and that the oft-repeated figure of 40,000 prostitutes converging on Germany for the FIFA World Cup is a gross exaggeration.'

Despite - or perhaps because - of the hype, German statistics on the total number of confirmed cases of "human trafficking for the purpose of sexual exploitation" in 2006 are readily available. For the entire country (not only sites around World Cup matches), for the entire year (not only the duration of the World Cup), what is the total? It's five. A monumentally unimpressive 0.0167 per cent of the predicted number that were supposed to occur during the World Cup alone.

This means either Germany's law enforcement can't be bothered to investigate crimes, or the predictions on sex trafficking produced for the delectation of the media are very far off the mark. I'm no expert on German police, but I know which option I'd put my money on.

The numbers don't hold up. They don't even sound likely, given the size of expected crowds at events like these. Consider the 40,000 meant to have been trafficked for the South Africa World Cup. With the expected number of fans going to the country estimated at 450,000, that just doesn't pass the sniff test. One working girl for every eleven people at the tournament?

As it happens, the claim about widespread sex tourism was refuted several months later when a UN Population Fund report showed sex workers' activity didn't go up at all.

The scare reports about projected trafficking and disease statistics were recycled in advance of the 2012 London Olympics, with conferences and fundraising events to 'raise awareness.' Early 2011 saw reports of the tens of thousands of women who were 'expected' to be trafficked into Dallas for fans of American football at the Super Bowl. The projected numbers were identical to those supposed to have been trafficked for the World Cup in South Africa, the Ryder Cup in Wales, the 2006 World Cup in Germany, the 2004 Olympics in Athens, and the 2000 Olympics in Sydney. Rio 2016 – the same stories again, this time with added fear of the zika virus. Summer 2017? Widespread claims that trafficking would be centered around areas in the solar eclipse path of full totality.

None of the projections have been supported by evidence beforehand nor proved to be accurate afterwards. Yet the same stories, the same numbers, and the usual suspects wanting money lurk behind every major sporting event of the last decade and longer.

Which is unsurprising because the entire 'World Cup' disease publicity was part of a strategy devised by Hunt Alternatives Fund to tie international sports headlines to hype about sex work and trafficking.

What is the Hunt Alternatives Fund? It is a private foundation started in the 1980s by Swanee Hunt - the daughter of right-wing US oil tycoon HL Hunt, a man who believed votes should be distributed to citizens according to their personal wealth.

Offshoots of HAF include Demand Abolition, a group that sources false information and distributes funding to a web of like-minded anti-sex work initiatives. Under these and many other names Hunt's billions are used to lobby for draconian developments in laws relating to prostitution.

Hunt Alternatives Fund's campaign attacking sex work was developed with the help of Abt Associates, one of the largest for-profit consulting firms in the world. Abt's other recent activities include accepting a $250 million consulting contract on how to improve health services in Nigeria, and another $121 million to look into the possibility of means-testing people on disability benefits in America.

Abt Associates' input resulted in an action plan that outlined the approach Hunt should take in promoting the criminalization of sex workers and clients. Rather than relying on hard research, they had a rather more flashy campaign in mind.

Here is a sample from Hunt's own report, Developing a National Action Plan for Eliminating Sex Trafficking: '[Hunt Alternatives Fund] should seize large marketing opportunities, such as the upcoming World Cup matches in South Africa, to create controversy on a world level and use it to draw attention to prostitution.' As a PR stunt, it worked. Speculative reports about tourism and prostitution were far more widely reported than the UN's evidence-based contradiction of these claims.

In the Hunt document these recommendations come under the heading of 'Demand Reduction as an Effective Public Health Intervention,' or in other words, push the myth that sex workers are responsible for STIs. But spreading rumours about disease is only one plan. Other sections cover 'Emphasizing Sexual Exploitation of Children Versus Adults' – so that's keeping the focus on child abuse, regardless of the actual issues – and 'Establish a National Center Devoted to Combating Demand,' since these recommendations would presumably do better with a 'centre' to give them legitimacy.

The Hunt/Abt strategy values lobbying above evidence. 'With severe time and resources constraints, lawmakers should not be asked to do the groundwork and raise support. Instead, a coalition and political advocates should present them with the issue, easily packaged and understood.' Also, never underestimate the power of celebrity: 'Several celebrities are already involved or interested in combating demand, such as Ashley Judd, Ashton Kutcher, and Demi Moore.'

Celebrity power is a huge tactic from the prohibition toolbox. Actresses like Anne Hathaway or Mira Sorvino who played sex workers once are feted as if their fictional experience bears any relationship to real life. Political celebs like Meryl Streep and Lena Dunham, in spite of zero qualifications, try to pressure Amnesty and other groups out of supporting sex workers. And people eat it up like they do all the other shallow, empty lifestyle pointers celebrity sells.

The Hunt guidelines note that finding evidence to support their viewpoint might be difficult. 'The point is that the "gold standard" usually is costly, and is not always feasible to pursue,' according to the document. 'The challenge in establishing standards of evidence is in determining the level or type of evidence required to convince [those organisations] sponsoring the programs.' Or, in other words, find the lowest acceptable level of evidence, and pursue only that. And, if in doubt, avoid conducting studies at all: 'No new information is necessarily required, so there is no need to wait for new research to unfold.'

Hunt Alternatives Fund declares that its main aim is to 'advance inclusive approaches to social change.' In case there was any doubt about how Hunt Alternatives Fund really feels about the people in sex work, and whether this 'inclusive change' extends to them, the guidelines speak for themselves. When discussing the words that should be used to describe people having sex for money, the document recommends sticking to 'prostituted person, sexually exploited, sex slaves.'

In Hunt's view, there is no way to distinguish between willing and unwilling sex workers, so why bother trying? 'When addressing demand that drives sexual slavery, it is not possible to separate the buyers of compelled sex from those whose participation is not due to force, fraud, or coercion.' This assumes that no participants in sex work have any agency. That solely by the act of having sex for money, one is rendered incapable of self-determination. That's a ludicrous assumption, with nothing to support it.

When the document says, 'If the National Campaign is to be comprehensive, it will require numerous partners from diverse backgrounds engaging in many different collective activities.' That presumably excludes all people who have a positive experience of sex work.

Hunt's involvement in stopping sex workers is so all-pervasive that it needs several guises. Demand Abolition is a Hunt project; so too is Cities Empowered Against Sexual Exploitation (CEASE) which has rolled out across the US. Swanee Hunt's deceased husband was a known client of escorts; whether his widow's abiding interest in punishing sex workers is due to some personal vendetta is impossible to confirm. The fact remains that her money buys an awful lot of bad science, harmful policy, and moral panic disguised as concern.

And those involved with Hunt can expect ample financial rewards. The Foundation's income in 2012 was over 12 million dollars; being a half-time advisor for the group pays over 100 grand in salary and benefits. Under "direct charitable activities," HAF say they spent $1,409,171 "eradicating the demand for purchased sex." While Swanee Hunt and family were the top donors, they also received one million dollars from Norway's Ministry of Foreign Affairs.

Hunt is not unusual. Shared Hope International (which campaigns against prostitution among other activities cleared $2,253,367 in 2011. The Coalition Against Trafficking in Women brought home $1,161,729 in 2012. Fireproof Ministries, which runs XXXChurch, netted $610,719 in 2011. $102,350 of this went into the pocket of Craig Gross. Shelley Lubben's Pink Cross Foundation raked in $137,183 in 2012. Of which half went to Shelley in salary and compensation. Melissa Farley (who has glowingly referred to sex workers as "house niggers") heads a group called Prostitution Research and Education, which pulled down $81,958 in 2012. To be clear: none of these groups offer direct front line services, legal aid, retraining programs, or shelter to affected women. What they do provide is very comfortable incomes to ideological partners in their anti-sex worker mission.

Looking over the list of beneficiaries of the Hunt Alternatives Fund, one sees many familiar names: Julie Bindel, Gail Dines, Melissa Farley. Conspicuously absent is input from sex workers themselves.

On Twitter I asked Julie Bindel if she found her alliance with Hunt to be a lucrative one – 'Absolutely lucrative as fuck!' was the reply. A 10-page consultation on prostitution that she wrote for the Glasgow City Council was funded to the tune of £20,000 (some four times what this book's UK advance came to). Catharine MacKinnon, a retired lawyer and radical feminist, has made over $100,000 *per year* speaking against sex workers. Ironic, isn't it, for opponents of sex work to be so pleased to be in it for the money?

Hunt Alternatives and Abt Associates are not the only groups using this kind of approach. The Schapiro Group, a market research firm in the US, regularly produces press releases with an anti-sex work bias. Their widely-debunked methods include counting photos of 'young looking girls' (whatever that means) on the internet. And their publications have been used to influence US policy on sex workers and advertising.

In September 2010, the popular website Craigslist was forced to remove its adult advertising section after explosive testimony to the US Congress. Deborah Richardson of the Women's Funding Network, which commissioned Schapiro to conduct the study, told legislators that juvenile prostitution is exploding at an astronomical rate. She laid the blame at the door of websites like Craigslist.

'An independent tracking study released today by the Women's Funding Network shows that over the past six months, the number of underage girls trafficked online has risen exponentially in three diverse states,' Richardson claimed. USA Today, the Houston Chronicle, the Miami Herald, and the Detroit Free Press all repeated the dire warnings as gospel.

What is the Schapiro Group? Perhaps it's easiest to explain that the Schapiro Group's other main activity is conducting 'push polls' for conservative candidates in the US. Push polling means cold-calling voters supposedly to assess their political leanings in an upcoming election, with the real agenda of 'pushing' a particular point of view.

Push polling is a strange business. It is also one I've experienced first-hand. As a poor student, I briefly worked in an establishment that used such tactics, and quit as soon as humanly possible. That call centre used every trick in the book, from misrepresenting ourselves, to lying about our location, to asking loaded questions. One I recall in particular was 'Would you be more, or less inclined to vote for the Democrat candidate if you knew he was involved in money laundering?' Of course, the man in question had never been accused of such a thing. The question was cleverly written to avoid a legal challenge, and also to invoke a particular response. That was the year of the surprise success of Republican House leader Newt Gingrich and his conservative 'Contract With America.' I was sickened to think my job had contributed to that in any way.

Considering the culture of push polling, it's no surprise that Schapiro's claims look frightening, until you critically assess the details. As with much push polling, definitions are stretched, and assumptions are relied upon. One study defined 'adolescents' as anyone up to the age of 22. Another focused on 'child sexual exploitation' of people several years over the age of consent.

Another study estimates the number of teenagers in escorting, but look carefully – they don't have any actual data on age. So, where do their numbers come from? Guesses of age, based on photos in escort ads! Even they admit this is bad data. 'The problem is, there is no scientifically reliable previous experience on which to base the probability that a girl selling sex who looks quite young is, indeed, under 18 years.' Doesn't stop them from writing a report in which they do exactly that.

There was no evidence that children were being exploited on Craigslist. Rather, the issue was used as a smokescreen to obtain the real desired result: eliminating consensual adult sex work. It's done by fudging the details and hiding behind the lie of protecting children – in much the same way the sexualization scare is used to push internet controls.

Meanwhile Polaris Project, which oversees the National Human Trafficking Resource Center's telephone hotlines, distributes press releases designed to stoke up moral panic. Such as the 2016 rash of stories about a 'national map' of 'underground sex slave bars' in the US. Their evidence for the data points on this fanciful map? Apparently, if you have ever been to "cantinas that charge excessively high prices for drinks," that means it's a sex slave network. Or something.

Polaris received $3.2 million in funding in 2010 for the National Human Traffic Resource Center - a phone tip line. According to their own documents, in that year 471 calls were received referencing potential human trafficking cases. In other words: the tip line is costing taxpayers about $7 grand per call. Almost none led to real trafficking convictions.

Groups like these present themselves as experts. Rather than report the truth, they peddle what others want to hear, creating a mirage of authority.

But why bother doing better? Shutting down websites and spreading misinformation is easier than doing the real work of stopping exploitation. Closing down Craigslist gets media attention. Hollywood stars fronting flashy awareness campaigns gets attention. High-profile raids, high-drama invented statistics, and Congressional hearings get attention. The real victims, wherever they may be, do not.

The Immigrant Council of Ireland (ICI), in 2009, released Globalization, Sex Trafficking and Prostitution: The Experiences of Migrant Women in Ireland. It contains many of the same problems as its UK counterparts. But what is even more questionable than the content are the people producing it.

The ICI was established by Sister Stanislaus Kennedy of The Religious Sisters of Charity, a Catholic order. As it turns out, The Religious Sisters of Charity have been involved with 'rehabilitating' women in prostitution for a long time. They (along with three other orders) helped run the asylums known as Magdalene Laundries in Ireland, the last of which closed in 1996.

The asylums were a system of long-term institutions for unacceptable women. Their remit expanded to include not only former prostitutes, but also unwed mothers, developmentally challenged women, and abused girls. Tens of thousands of inmates were made to do hard physical labor, and endured a daily regime of enforced prayer and silence.

In 1993 when one of the orders sold land to a developer. The remains of 155 inmates of the Magdalene Laundry were exhumed from an unmarked grave. Many former inmates of Laundries have testified to sexual, psychological, and physical abuse that occurred within the asylums.

The Commission to Inquire into Child Abuse published the Ryan report in 2009. In the report, survivor accounts of Magdalene Laundries describe abuse that amounted to slavery. Considering how recently the scandal broke, it's horrifying to see the same groups scoop up government grants on sex work and trafficking.

ICI's track record, and that of the associated charity Ruhama, does not point to major success. A July 2011 report, Who are Ireland's brothel keepers? detailed arrests from 2008 to 2011. According to their own statistics, 91% of the people convicted were sex workers, not owners or managers of brothels who have others working for them. Data collected by Uglymugs IE, a sex worker-led group, found the stats from 2008 to 2013 confirmed this was not unusual. 92.9% of the people arrested under Ireland's laws – meant to punish pimps, traffickers, and all the other baddies – end up imprisoning sex workers themselves.

Freedom Of Information Act requests show sex workers fined and given criminal records with the money going to the ICI, Ruhama, and other anti-sex worker groups.[cv] Putting women in jail is not "rescue," not by any stretch of the imagination. Stuffing the pockets of known abusers like the Magdalene orders doesn't help, either. They are literally the ones profiting off of prostitution. Who are the real pimps again?

As far as these groups are concerned, the thin research they push and damaging results they obtain is good enough for them.

'There is no "other side"' of the argument,' sneers Hunt. In spite of evidence that 60 per cent people think prostitution should be the choice of the person doing it, not the government. 'They have no credible supporters,' claims Hunt. Who's calling whom not credible? When HAF admits in its own reports to promoting minimal research standards and celebrity endorsement over intellectually honest evidence.

Charities and other groups which purport to 'attack' the problem of sex work and 'save' the victims of trafficking are little different. For all the good work they purport to do, there is also a network of high-profile campaigns, conferences, and media-friendly PR that eats up rather a lot of the money donated – including money given by the government.

£100,000 was given by the British government to the Poppy Project for victims identified by Pentameter Two – on top of the over £2 million it received in funding and the £5.8 million overall given to its parent project, Eaves. At the time of the operation, their facilities in London included fewer than twenty beds. Twenty seems a low number if they expected the police to find thousands of trafficked women. Of course, the operation only identified two victims, so it was not a problem.

A detailed report in Truthout[cvi] revealed that the fifty largest anti-trafficking organizations in the United States have an estimated income of about $700 million per year, as of 2015. If they were a country this would give them the world's 184th largest GDP just above Samoa. It could be more, given that a third of them do not release public financial records. Add in the top 40 groups funded by the US State Department not already on that list, and the combined budgets top $1.2 billion. This is only the tip of the iceberg as far as funding is concerned.

Groups receiving funds are not made to collect data, nor prove the existence of a local trafficking problem before securing grants. It was January 2008 before task forces were required to report any activity to the US Bureau of Justice Statistics, and it is still incomplete (and in many cases, current only to the 2012 financial year).

When it comes to victims saved, we know a bit more. Federal trafficking investigations in 2012 totaled 2,398 cases.[cvii] The Department of Justice charged against 200 defendants and convicted 138 traffickers: that's $8.6 million, minimum, per conviction.

How is it possible for so much money to result in so few convictions? These groups have few restrictions on how their funds can be used. For instance, it would be acceptable for a group to, say, purchase 'designated vehicles' and fund 'deputy' positions even without a single reported victim in the community. A lot also goes to 'awareness raising,' which typically consists of billboards, posters, talks in schools, and sending delegates to international conferences.

If you look on Twitter, for example you'll notice that in the US alone there are more accounts for groups supposedly raising awareness of trafficking than there are *actual documented victims*. The money is literally going to groups to tweet amongst themselves. *Missing: The Complete Saga* is a video game funded by prohibitionists where you can 'play' a trafficked child in India. Who is helped by this? The short answer: no one.

In 2011, Iowa senator Chuck Grassley called for action after audits showed human trafficking groups reporting questionable costs. The audits showed of the $8.24 million total the Department of Justice awarded to six grant recipients, there was $2.72 million in unsupported, unallowable, or questioned costs.[cviii]

The Heartland Alliance for Human Needs in Chicago, which was awarded $2 million, spent $902,122 on salaries and $174,479 for 'fringe benefits' which did not have appropriate authorisation. A 2008 audit found although the Office of Justice Programs' human grant recipients have 'built significant capacities to serve victims,' the programs have not 'identified and served significant numbers of victims.'

Also in 2011, Denise Marshall, chief executive of Eaves Housing for Women and the Poppy Project in the UK (which funds Lilith R&D, of the fake lap dancing statistics), handed back a medal she received from the Queen in 2007. Marshall said it was in protest at funding cuts. 'We have always worked on a shoestring, but now that shoestring has been cut,' said Marshall in an interview.

The shoestring Marshall refers to included £1.95 million of government funding in 2010, which was awarded to the Salvation Army instead. Government funding made up only some of Eaves' funding. In 2010 their income, according to the Charities Commission website, was about £5.4 million. They launched a new fundraising drive to recover some of the funds lost from the government grants, as well.

The biggest overhead for Eaves/Poppy is not the services provided, but salaries. Of the 117 people who work for Eaves, eighty are volunteers. The thirty-seven paid staff received £2.9 million – more than half the total budget – in 2010. If divided equally, that's £78,378.38 per paid staff member to cover salary, National Insurance contributions, etc.

Surely the main thing is that resources are going directly to the women they're helping. According to papers filed by Eaves with the Charities Commission, only £476,231 went to 'service user costs' – less than a tenth of their income.

Eaves claimed the decision to hand trafficking funding to the Salvation Army forced them to drop fourteen staff members. It's unclear whether they mean paid or unpaid ones, but assuming paid, Eaves could have absorbed the loss if the average staff provision was £58,000 –more than double the average London salary.

Huge salaries in this sector are common. A part-time job at Hunt Alternatives Fund paid one advisor $101,562 in salary and benefits.

Some objected to the Salvation Army getting the government's trafficking grant, but Eaves only had a presence in London while the Salvation Army is nationwide. The Sally Army provide services for both men and for women, and victims of non-sex trafficking. Eaves' facilities for victims –fewer than twenty beds – were accessible only to women, only to sex trafficked victims, and only if they agreed to contribute to police investigations. For plenty of reasons (not least potential threats to relatives in their home countries) many genuine trafficking victims do not wish to do this.

It's not only Eaves that operates more in the realm of PR than reality. In 2016 ex-employees of trafficking charity Courage House in California started to go public with a history of inadequate staffing, failure to protect residents' privacy, and more abuses. Violations of local codes forced the facility to close its doors. While the well-paid founder, Jenny Williamson, rubbed shoulders with the likes of Julianne Moore and Eva Longoria, improvements that were promised to donors were kicked into the long grass. Even after the group home shut, Williamson continued accepting high-profile donations from people unaware of it status.[cix]

At the height of its operation, Courage House had the capacity to house just six girls all while the founder enjoyed in millions in grants and donations. According to Reason magazine, government grants alone netted the organization over *nine thousand dollars* per girl per month.[cx] The Courage House website still mentions its 'international' outreach in California and Tanzania – a country selected, perhaps, for its less stringent oversight of group homes and charities?

There are also the academics, researchers, and writers who earn their living not through hands-on effort, but by attracting grant funding or setting themselves up in tenured college lectureships. And it can be very lucrative. Catherine MacKinnon's base salary at the University of Michigan (speaking engagements, writing, and tours) was $273,000 in 2009. In 2010 the university paid her $280,000, again excluding all the pay and perks that come with her speaking tours. This is over twenty times what the average sex worker earns in the US annually.

The website Fundingtrends.org, a US-based site, shows trends in research grants funded since 1991. It processes project funding data from the US National Institutes of Health (NIH), European Commission (EC), Canadian and Australian research councils, and many others. It also includes keywords from MEDLINE article abstracts, forming an overview of what kinds of research are being funded, and the amounts involved.

Funding for studying trafficking is a growth area. From almost nothing in 1991, it was funded worldwide by 2010 to the tune of 600 million US dollars, according to Fundingtrends.org. (The amount practically double from 2005 to 2007.) This is a total greater than the amount of grant money to study lung cancer, which affects far more people. By the end of 2016, the value of grants awarded for trafficking amounted to double the money offered for lung cancer. Spending on trafficking since 2000 has dwarfed the academic awards on important international health concerns like malnutrition, malaria, or tuberculosis – conditions that kill millions of people annually worldwide, and affect hundreds of millions more. Funding for trafficking research is not only greater than each of these, it's 20 times greater than all of the funding for these health crises combined. Remember: this is for research only. It does not include other sources of funding, namely donations wrung out of the impressionable public, government awards, and law enforcement programs.

This trend has happened at the same time mentions of trafficking started to become interesting to the media. News database searches showed there were only three references to 'human trafficking' or 'trafficking in humans' before 2000. It was mentioned 9 times in 2000 and 41 times in 2001. Use of these terms in the news reached 100 mentions for the first time in 2005. In 2010, there were more than 500 references. Since then? Tens of thousands. The money made available to tackle these problems is through the roof. But the number of confirmed victims and prosecutable cases hasn't gone up at all.

Undeterred, news organizations have continued to produce biased and untrue claims – such as when Holly Baxter in the *Guardian* claimed 80% of Vietnamese migrants in the UK were also nail technicians by day, and secretly trafficked sex workers by night. The paper had to rapidly make corrections and even issue a 'fact check' on their own piece for this jaw-dropping bit of numerical illiteracy, not to mention racism.

On social media Baxter doubled down and defended her claims. Her source for this ludicrous number? A half-remembered article in some other paper that hadn't even been correctly quoted. The Guardian was forced to issues a fact check and apology directly related to her claims. In spite of this, her error riddled claims were later widely referenced by anti-trafficking charities. (Baxter later became a deputy editor at the *Independent*, where anti-sex worker pieces by Julie Bindel are consistently commissioned.)

In March 2017, a conference in the UK announced that banks had been using personal customer data to 'identify' victims of trafficking. Their criteria? They were looking for women from Eastern Europe who had ever bought condoms. The women flagged by these scattershot operations can no doubt expect harassment from the Home Office for the crime of looking after their own sexual health.

The report on banks also revealed some imaginative 'insights' on the trafficked. According to news reports, banks also looked for women who used their accounts twice in the same day, perhaps 'high end restaurants and cheap diners on the same day' in the belief that they could spot a sex worker dining with her client while a pimp eats more frugally nearby.

This is Inspector Clouseau-level nonsense. What sex worker ever paid for her own 'high end' date? Much less that as well as the food her manager, if any, eats? The least bit of logic applied to these algorithms should reveal that the banks have bought a tall tale about sex workers hook, line, and sinker. And we can assume some group or consultant was paid very well for the privilege of making up such utter fiction.

With their heads stuck firmly in ideology instead of reality, self-appointed experts respond to the inconvenient truth not by adjusting their beliefs but by creating "alternative facts." Over and again the factually-challenged echo chamber driving this agenda disseminates bunk data. Skewed statistics and biased media reports are vital to the process. Consider why the issue of trafficking is seldom seen from the migrant's point of view – a point of view in which cops are not heroes, and laws that claim to "save" them equal deportation and abuse.

Trafficking orgs push sensational narratives, roping in celebrities in a way that is irresistible to media and policymakers. Most of these celebs are neither knowledgeable nor accurate in their efforts. Worst of all? There is no evidence that public service campaigns make any difference to trafficking convictions. Quite the opposite: after viewing such material, people feel 'satisfied' they have done something to help even when they have done nothing at all.

While Hollywood has long supported AIDS crisis charities, they seem to turn a blind eye to the prohibitionist policy that forces HIV orgs to support full criminalization of sex work, or else give up US funding. This is, in no uncertain terms, a harm reduction crisis – especially given the overlaps of the most at-risk groups involved. Men who have sex with men and IV drug users are simply pawns in a game that revolves entirely around manufacturing misleading images of kidnapped girls.

Perhaps President Trump's endorsement of trafficking crackdowns will change the minds of the people pushing these pointless, harmful campaigns? Already the signs point to no: the Irish agency Ruhama teamed up with the US Department of Homeland Security in March 2017 to discuss the 'problem' of migrant workers at a conference. Ivanka Trump's speech to the UN in September 2017, repeating many myths, was lauded by groups in spite of her clothing company having been revealed to use cheap Chinese labor of 60 hours a week for $62 pay.[cxi] They are no doubt hoping to do exactly what the US political establishment has done and kiss the ass of whoever's on charge not because they are ethical or correct, but because they're popular.

Is it any surprise? Like Trump, anti-trafficking campaigns put opponents on the back foot with a constant barrage of untruth. And as much as these groups claim to detest the current administration, they are unlikely to criticize what has to date been a lucrative income as pimps of the Rescue Industry.

CHAPTER 6

Did You Know...

- *The "Swedish Model" is not decriminalization*
- *Anti-sex work campaigns recruit and heavily coach survivors while ignoring their real stories*

Jannine fits every stereotype. Abused in childhood and by her current partner. Drug habit. She works on the street to fund her habit.

In 2007 the Scottish Parliament passes the Prostitution (Public Places) Act, outlawing curb-crawling. Jannine's clients are now breaking the law. If she worked indoors, this would not be the case. But her addiction keeps her from being able to hold down shifts in indoor sex work.

As she drinks a hot chocolate and takes a handful of free condoms, Jannine talks about the previous night to an outreach worker. She was out for hours trying avoid police, who will scare her clients away, while going through withdrawal. She missed her hostel's curfew and had to sleep at a bus stop in the dead of winter.

When Jannine is stopped by the police, she can't expect sympathy. There's a serial rapist going around but she is taking her chances because there are few clients. "I used to complain about having to come out here to work," she tells the outreach worker. "I had *nothing* to complain about compared to now." Jannine knows the difference between a bad situation and a worse one.

Research backs up what Jannine already knows to be true: after being displaced by police, sex workers are pressured into riskier work practices[cxii] and lose access to outreach and health services.[cxiii] They experience double the amount of violence from clients[cxiv] - even senior police officers admit "operations to tackle the trade are counterproductive & likely to put women's lives at risk."[cxv]

It's years later that Jannine's story becomes known, blogged by the outreach worker whose services had to close due to lack of funding. What happened to Jannine? No one knows. Most likely nothing good.

Those whose primary goal is to 'send a message' prioritize ideology over safety for people who don't have good choices. They force people in the margins to fall through the cracks. They don't understand how bad is still better than worse. They block out dissent and force through harmful laws, while pushing stereotypes. The majority of sex workers who are attacked cite hostility and prejudice as the reasons they were targeted.[cxvi]

This does no favours for women like Jannine. The campaigners are not staffing the drop-in vans or homeless shelters where women like Jannine are found. They are at international conferences in 5-star resorts, talking about feminist theory and being 'a voice for the voiceless.'

The mistakes made over and again by lobbyists and policymakers come from a failure to listen to the people with the most at stake: sex workers themselves.

The varied experiences of sex workers are disregarded when considering 'what to do' about them. It's easy to see why people are uncomfortable with experiences like Jannine's. But to not listen to how new laws affect her is equivalent to driving away from the scene of an accident. The current fad for promoting the so-called 'Swedish Model' is but one example.

Sweden's 1999 law that criminalizes the buying of sex has been shown conclusively not to eradicate sex work.[cxvii] But more to the point: its supporters claim it decriminalizes prostitutes, harming only the "pimps and johns." This is untrue.

Sex workers from countries where these laws have been brought in say over and again how the laws make their conditions of work worse. How the government treats them like wards of the state, harasses them for evidence against their clients, and in extreme cases – like the murder of Petite Jasmine – actively puts their lives at risk. In Norway, police call their harassment of sex workers "Operation Homeless." This is not, and can never be, beneficial to women.

Yet sex workers are ignored, belittled, and excluded from the discussion. Such input is negated by journalists and lobbyists who call sex workers "orifices". Or supposed feminists Caroline Criado-Perez and Sarah Ditum speculating online that sperm makes your brain stop working (really). They endlessly hand-wring about whether punters respect sex workers, when they themselves clearly do not!

Supporters of the Swedish Model claim it's decrim, even when the records of women arrested for loitering or solicitation are not scrubbed. The penalties in law against the sex workers are never removed. The supporters of this model do not campaign to get sex workers off of sex offender registries, or offer career alternatives beyond sweatshop training. It isn't decriminalisation – but nice middle-class ladies couldn't possibly be trying to mislead the public, now could they? They wibble on about how bad legalization is – a fact sex worker-led organizations not only know, but knew before anyone else did. They falsely claim that legalization is what sex workers want, no matter how many times workers say actually, decriminalization is better and safer. They keep talking about Amsterdam and the Bunny Ranch because the truth (most sex workers do not want to work there) is inconvenient. They keep the focus on client review boards because the truth (many service providers are not respected by their customers) does not suit their agenda.

Part of the problem is how different groups define 'trafficked.' To many, the assumption was that if someone was not a citizen and working in the sex trade, she must be trafficked. That's quite a leap in logic! I worked in the sex trade in the UK. I was born somewhere else. Does that mean I was 'trafficked'? According to that methodology: yes.

The Poppy Project reported in 2004 that 80 per cent of prostitutes in London flats were foreign-born. There is no evidence those women were trafficked or that this proportion applies to the entire UK. (The UK-wide percentage of foreign born sex workers is 37 per cent.)

If that still sounds high, keep in mind 'foreign-born' includes citizens of other EU countries, who have the right to work in the UK. Not that these are even reported accurately. Eaves, the organisation that includes the Poppy Project, did an interesting nip-and-tuck on reporting the origins of women working in the sex trade in London. In their 2004 report *Sex in the City*, they claimed 25 per cent of women working in London were from Eastern Europe. But look closer – they have classified Italy and Greece as 'Eastern European' countries. [cxviii]

The reason is given that 'because these ethnicities are often used to code women from the Balkan region, advised by pimps and traffickers to lie about their ethnicity to avoid immigration issues.' Hey, my dad is Italian … if I said this to a researcher, would they assume I'm lying, and am really Eastern European? Again: yes, according to that methodology.

It is interesting to see groups like Eaves using prejudice against Eastern Europeans to support their claims. (Prejudice that is now so rampant in the UK, a Polish man was kicked to death in the streets of Essex by a group of British teenagers, for being foreign.)

Racism and xenophobia underpins much of the trafficking narrative. It's consistently used worldwide: from images showing young white girls being manhandled by dark-skinned men, to the repeated Donald Trump claims about "Mexican rapists" in the 2016 US presidential election. In the UK, child sexual abuse (which is statistically far more likely to happen within a family) is now presented in the media as something only "roving Islamic gangs" do. So-called radical feminists have no problem taking advantage of this racist narrative – even, when it suits them, forming coalitions with the members of the Family Research Council and other known extremist groups.

The more we are forced to engage with alternative facts, the more we are vulnerable to these intellectual grifters. The more fake experts influence policy, the more damage they do. For migrant sex workers like me, being told that our input doesn't count and we are incorrect about things we actually experienced – it's gaslighting pure and simple.

By keeping the focus on the trafficking panic, instead of sex workers who are adults working in the country where they were born, they exclude the majority of sex workers. By claiming migrants and underage are incapable of speaking for themselves or otherwise 'hidden,' they silence those voices, too.

There are women like Jannine for whom sex work is the best of a set of poor choices. There are also women who see sex work as a stopgap, a stepping stone to something else.

Today, few Eastern Europeans could be tricked to enter the sex industry – they know it is an option. Ports like Odessa, in southern Ukraine, have witnessed an above-ground boom in sex services. 'An experienced girl gets off the plane covered in gold, diamonds and furs, and goes back to her home village,' says psychologist Svetlana Chernolutskaya in an interview with *Time* magazine. 'She tells them how much money they can make turning tricks in a foreign country.'[cxix]

US diplomatic cables confirm that would-be rescuers hoping for glory in Armenia would be disappointed by the reality. 'We went to Vanadzor expecting to hear stories of illicit smuggling across borders and of girls lured into prostitution under false pretenses. What we heard was significantly more pedestrian ... And while the prostitutes and the NGO employees we met said sometimes women are abused in the brothels, or aren't paid in full, they said the greater part of women generally understand what they are getting themselves into, and may already have worked as prostitutes for years.'[cxx]

'Reporters always come here demanding to see the victims,' says Olga Kostyuk, deputy head of a charity in Odessa, Ukraine. 'They want to see the men, the pimps, the manipulators behind all of this. But things are not so simple now.'

That hasn't stopped Western media from trying to wring more mileage out of the story regardless. In 2008, an ITV programme related the tale of a fourteen-year-old girl sold for sex at a petrol station in Romania. The problem was, it wasn't true. The woman was actually twenty-five years old and a career sex worker.

In the report, also broadcast on CNN, a journalist claimed Monica Ghinga's identification papers proved she was fourteen years old. The reporter met with alleged traffickers, saying he would pay €800 for her and take the girl to London. Romanian police discovered the truth when they investigated the incident. Ghinga admitted that she lied about her age to the television crew and agreed to have sex with them for one night.[cxxi]

The ITV debacle was one in a string of high-profile trafficking failures. In 2014, Somaly Mam, a Cambodian trafficking survivor beloved of celebrities such as Susan Sarandon and Sheryl Sandberg, was revealed not to have been either trafficked or a sex worker at any point in her past.

Another tall tale was the story of Long Pros, whose sad background was promoted by Mam's foundation: the one-eyed girl had not had her eye gouged out by an angry pimp, as was once claimed. Her parents revealed it was surgically removed following a childhood illness.

These were only the tip of the iceberg as far as Mam's organisation went; *El Mundo*, the second largest paper in Spain, revealed a culture of sloppy financial paperwork as well as allegations of sexual abuse and harassment by employees. The industry attracts its fair share of abusers, from Dan Benedict of the Defender Foundation who has ties to white supremacy groups and child abuse convictions on his record, to California's Rescue Children From Human Trafficking Foundation which is run by a con artist who pretended to be a European royal.

In Thailand, Mickey Choothesa and COSA (Children's Organization of Southeast Asia), was a nonprofit organization and shelter founded in 2006 to provide sanctuary, shelter and education. But as documentary filmmakers discovered when they went to visit the shelter, another scam. Tales of parents selling their children gained millions in donations for a shelter that did not exist at all.[cxxii] Mikael Alfven, founder of the charity Love and Hope, was accused of coaching young women in Nepal to fabricate sex trafficking stories – because, he said, it would increase donations from the Swedish public.[cxxiii]

The award-winning film *Eden*, which purported to be the story of a trafficked woman (Chong Kim) forced into prostitution in the US, also turned out to be fabricated. Years of footwork by activist Mistress Matisse uncovered that the film's lurid tale of rape, murder, and kidnapping was untrue. Breaking Out, an anti-trafficking organisation that supported Kim, withdrew their association when their internal audits failed to find any truth in her story.

In Ireland, a 28-year-old Australian con artist named Samantha Azzopardi posed as a trafficked teenager unable to speak English, kicking off a media furore. The frantic search for her 'abusers' cost the state over 350,000 Euros. On her return to her homeland, she posed as a 13-year-old and was placed in foster care in Sydney. Over $10,000 in charity handouts later she was arrested and sent to prison for 10 years for fraud. It later emerged she had been deported from Canada years earlier after falsely claiming to be an abused teenager.

In Holland, 'Patricia Perquin' claimed to have been a trafficked woman working in Amsterdam's famous red light district. She was later revealed as a discredited journalist named Valerie Lempereur. Her story didn't add up when other women in the RLD pointed out the working details were wrong and number of clients she claimed to have serviced in the highly regulated industry there was ten times too high. It was later discovered she had been working as a writer in Belgium during the dates she claimed to be in the RLD.[cxxiv]

Other people who claim to have been trafficked find their stories eagerly seized upon by the rescue industry, only to be cast aside when they no longer perform up to expectations. Stella Marr, a blogger who claimed to have been a call girl in Manhattan kept captive by her pimp, spun intriguing tales of seeing other sex workers shot in the face. She toured the world talking about her experiences and promoting the continued criminalization of sex work. When it was later revealed she was the wife of a high-profile nuclear scientist, and none of her stories about her time in New York City could be confirmed, her benefactors dropped her like a hot potato.

Overseas the situation happens again and again. Justine Reilly, a spokesperson for Ruhama, appeared on Irish television over the years in a number of guises. Whether she was calling herself "Mary," "Marian," or "Lisa," Reilly's refusal to change her distinctive platinum cornrows meant she was exposed as the same person giving 'evidence of trafficking' under multiple names. Worse still – she had been convicted of pimping. Once her real identity became common knowledge, she was dumped from Ruhama and SPACE International. In 2017 a dating profile for Justine was spotted on Tinder. Her self-declared occupation? Actress.

Reilly's former SPACE business partner Rachel Moran is another. Moran became a streetwalker in Ireland in her teens and later authored an account of her experiences. While some sex workers in Dublin at the time claimed never to have met her, her book became a bestseller there. It emerged that money donated to her charity by Coalition Against

Trafficking in Women had gone into her personal account. As years wore on, she was sidelined – rumors abounded of unpredictable behaviour as the result of addiction problems. Whatever the truth, it is fair to say she was not getting the treatment she needed and instead was used as the show pony of a movement cared little for her well-being.

I did meet Rachel briefly once, during a debate in a pub hosted by Rupert Everett. She said, on camera, that all sex workers were "better off dead." All I could do was mumble 'where there's life there's hope' in utter shock. It is sad to think she truly believes that, and worse to know she endorses policies that will guarantee more deaths.

Jill Brenneman, who was kidnapped and trafficked as a teenager, was another lured into representing anti-sex work organizations. However she realized early on that they were as exploitative as the man who had abducted and abused her, and later became an advocate for sex workers' rights. Leaving the people who claimed to want to "rescue" her resulted in hate mail and death threats.

Amber Paulina of Seattle described her experience. Church elders in a rescue organization, with no qualifications, opened a facility for trafficked girls. She was told to call the director "Mom" and her husband "Dad" and they called all the girls their "daughters." Amber was grilled about her masturbation habits and was forced to write book reports on "famous" survivors like Rachel Lloyd while the "family" received conference invitations and international accolades.

"I made bracelets ... that were flipped over at nine bucks a pop en masse at anti-trafficking events and at local boutiques. All material donated. 'Made by trafficking survivor' bracelets. All the time. For money. Unpaid," Amber says.

Laura LeMoon, who also identifies as a trafficking survivor, confirms this in an article for *We Are Your Voice* magazine. "People outed me without my permission ... the rampant abuse of power runs throughout the entire anti-trafficking field right now."

Laura also interviews Desiree, who worked in the Midwest as a human trafficking program coordinator, and was fired for being a survivor. Desiree says, "[The executive director] found out I was a survivor. She would tell me things like ... 'trafficking survivors are manipulative,' 'well, HT [human trafficking] survivors are criminals, so...' "

Perhaps the most detailed account of what goes on within the anti-sex work community came from one of its own. Beth Brigham, a former graduate student mentored by anti-prostitution lecturer Gail Dines, revealed in great detail what it was like working for the woman herself:

Dines describes sexual attackers as being capable of smelling out "seasoned" victims. "Seasoning" is a term for the theory that after someone is assaulted, subconscious mannerisms and actions present in the survivor that send a signal to sexual predators that they are more vulnerable than others and therefore more easy targets ...

What I didn't realize until later was that what Dines had smelled out my "seasoning." Because she was offering me this explanation for why I felt like the world was against me, I began taking her word as my ultimate truth.

Before long, I was her paid assistant. She took note of my persuasiveness, outgoing nature, and skill with the crafting of words. At twenty years old, I was a natural leader. And before long, I was doing everything from her research to traveling with her to attend the lectures she told me I would one day be giving in her place.

The entire story is heartbreaking, and ends with Beth cast out from Dines's inner circle, academic dreams in tatters, for daring to question anything about her professor. Beth later became a fetish model and blogger advocating for rights for sex workers. Her account is disturbing not least because the very kind of gaslighting she describes Dines doing to her students? Is exactly what Dines and others like her accuse pimps of doing to keep sex workers under control.

The simplistic "solution" often served up is that creating a black market will somehow make black markets disappear. Or stopping how sex workers vet clients, and shutting down their support, will make paid sex stop. Close Backpage, eliminate funding from harm reduction charities, and presto! It will all just go away.

If only it was as simple as that.

Meenu Seshu, founder of SANGRAM, a peer education organization for sex workers in India, summarizes the situation: 'The community is never ever going to respond to anybody who is bringing in the police to rescue them, because they do not view that as a "rescue". They view that as another oppressive thing that's done to them.'[cxxv]

In Cambodia, the government began targeting the sex industry with its 2008 Law on Suppression of Human Trafficking and Sexual Exploitation. A survey found that less than 1 per cent of sex workers in Cambodia were sold into prostitution.[cxxvi] The trafficking panic has nonetheless overshadowed the human rights of Cambodian sex workers – with deadly results.

Organizations battling HIV in Cambodia say the law is driving sex workers underground, limiting access to health services. Women who worked in brothels avoid the raids by using 'indirect' venues like karaoke bars, where clients take them off-site. This opens the door to abuse and health risks. According to Tony Lisle from UNAIDS, 'the crackdowns create difficulties for HIV prevention organizations to reach those who are most at risk, particularly sex workers.'[cxxvii]

Reports from Human Rights Watch confirm that the arrests do not locate trafficked women, and that those rounded up are raped by police and government officials, before being thrown in prison.[cxxviii] Research in 2015 demonstrated the breakdown of safety and peer networks among sex workers, leading to increased stigma and risk.[cxxix]

A diplomatic cable from 2006 confirms this. It also shows that the situation has been known for some time. 'Targeting sex workers alone is not a viable solution to ridding Cambodia of prostitution nor is it particularly effective in addressing trafficking in persons. The fact that no pimps or brothel owners have been held responsible after the raids on nine brothels raises questions as to the government's motivations.' [cxxx]

In September 2017 Julie Bindel released a new text claiming to tell all sides. Unlike her previous efforts this was aimed more at a scholarly market than a popular one, with aspirations to be a summary of investigations into sex workers' organizations. The newspaper coverage was unescapable in the run-up to its release, with Bindel herself penning vicious invectives against sex workers in all the major papers.

Bindel initially crowdfunded the book to the tune of £7000. Backers could pay £250 for the honor of having lunch with the woman herself. Ironic when criminalized sex workers are also often forced to advertise their services as "lunch dates". On top of this, the book had an advance from Palgrave, so her punters end up paying twice.

The title 'The Pimping of Prostitution,' is ironic given anti-sex work crusades demonstrably attract and spend far more money than shoestring operations like rights orgs do. It was offered at an eye-watering $39.99 for the paperback ($37.99 for Kindle). But while supporters paid a premium for the content, does the book deliver?

In a word: no. While advertised as a scholarly work it lacks any academic rigor. Most of the references are self-citations of privately published reviews written by Bindel and Melissa Farley. Peer review? What peer review? Unsurprising, given Bindel's most famous quote is that if given a gun and forced to choose between shooting a pimp and an academic, she would shoot the academic.

Her research partner Melissa Farley is little better, mind, given a portion of her research website is given over to making jokes about sex workers like "I became a prostitute because I saw Pretty Baby and it reminded me of my stepfather and I thought I could get paid for it … I realized that gang rape could be a transcendental experience." Yes, that's right – jokes about incest and rape. Classy.

Bindel claims to have interviewed 250 people in 40 countries about sex work - by her own admission they are journalist friends of hers, police, and 'regular members of the public who knew very little, if anything, about the sex trade.' If this was a middle school project it would be laughed out of class for its utter lack of quality.

She notes in acknowledgments that 'the other side' trusted her to 'represent their words and views fairly.' Is that so? She has called legalization and decriminalization the same thing when they are not. Despite being told many times sex workers support decriminalization, not legalization, Julie is too dishonest to admit this, setting up a straw (wo)man and knocking it down over and over.

A lengthy part is given over to advancing conspiracy theories involving billionaire financier George Soros. Anti-Semitic attacks on Soros are such a staple of the far right I won't duplicate them here, but it is shocking – or *should be* shocking, though given Brexit and Trump perhaps not so much in 2017 – to read a supposedly mainstream feminist giving airtime to this level of hate speech.

She has not so much interviewed her opponents as hand-selected people uninvolved in activism or sex work. Why are her lengthy conversations with Peter Tatchell about gay men and the age of consent here, if not to stoke pedophilia fears on the back of homophobia? It seemed like a non sequitur until I heard that in the late 80s, Julie Bindel picketed the HIV and sexual health charity Terrence Higgins Trust on the grounds it was taking state money away from women's charities. And even today, she accuses AIDS organizations of being in the "pimp lobby" for trying to overturn gagging rules that strip their funding if they don't condemn and criminalize sex workers.[1]

Why does she place so much importance on tearing down sociologist Dr Catherine Hakim, whose area of research this is not? How is politician Keith Vaz's relationship with male escorts related to violence against women? How does Bindel's friend Rachel Moran tweeting 'cock' at the director of Amnesty International advance their cause, and why is this the epigram of a chapter as if it is philosophical gold from the mouth of a scholar? (And why are Palgrave printing it?) It all amounts to

---

[1] I feel obliged to note, here, that Ms Bindel's solicitor threatened a libel lawsuit when this book appeared. However, given the reliability of my source and Bindel's own words in *Newsweek* in September 2017, not to mention my distaste for people who believe libel tourism is a suitable reaction to hurt feelings, I am satisfied to let the sentences stand.

a bunch of unconnected hit jobs padding out a shoddy book. The rest is a collection of personal anecdotes, old feminists she once met, and so on. She details the time in the 70s she was pen-friends with imprisoned sex worker Emma Humphreys, while dodging the question of why the laws she supports would still put women like Emma in jail.

When discussing sex workers condescension drips from every word and it is clear she is used to having the floor to herself. Unable to take criticism or debate (the launch party for her book at "independent intellectual venue" Conway Hall expressly forbade sex work activists), disgusted by the humans she so profitably claims to save. In fact, it is nearly indistinguishable from Kat Banyard's recent polemic *The Pimp State*, which also only mentions sex workers to ridicule them. This schtick would be funny if it didn't have repercussions on real lives.

Not to mention, the coded racism Bindel uses by invoking the word *pimp* over and over. Why not manager or boss, as sex workers normally call the people they work for? Because pimp has other layers. It's a dog whistle meant to indicate to us a class of violent black men in control of women.

Independent sex workers who organize their own affairs and work solo. Roommates who share a flat and both happen to sell sex. Managers running escorts agencies with a dozen or so girls they mostly interact with by text. Massage parlor owners. Women whose house is used by other sex workers, so technically I guess are madams. People who set up message boards and internet forums where clients and sex workers talk among themselves and with each other. All of these are people who get called "pimps" by the anti-sex lobby.

Occasionally you also hear talk of the "Eastern European gangmaster", but for some reason the class- and racially-evocative term "pimp" comes up far, far more often. Could that be because plain xenophobia just doesn't inspire the troops in quite the same way bald racism does?

The anti-sex lobby's fantasy use of the term "pimp" is bogus and it is racist. Anyone who claims otherwise is being purposely disingenuous for the sake of striking fear into white, English-speaking, middle-class people.

But the main takeaway from the book is its desperation. The money she raised appears to have gone towards an all-expenses-paid international jaunt with only the slenderest of results to show for it. The text reads less like a new movement and more like a last gasp. If this is Bindel's final shot at the history books then let it also be her epitaph. Here lies prohibition: illogical, illiberal, and entirely without merit.

Even strident opponents of sex work seem confused about whether their approach even works. In a 2003 article, Julie Bindel admitted that making sex work illegal does more harm than good. Here's the twist that flipped her script: the buyers were women.

In a piece on female sex tourists in the Dominican Republic, she notes: 'There are obvious differences between female and male sex tourism ... they [are not] vulnerable to criminalization, unlike female prostitutes whose activities are illegal.' [cxxxi] My jaw hit the floor to realize Bindel knows full well that criminalization does indeed play a part in making sex workers vulnerable.

Others demonstrate a naivety about economic reality that is almost touching in its innocence. Catherine Redfern writes that '[n]o one should be forced to do any kind of work that they really don't want to do, simply to survive.'[cxxxii] Which is amazing given that the majority of all waged work is done for exactly that reason. How many people restocking the shelves in Walmart are there because it's what they always dreamed of doing?

Most people have to work to earn a living. In my experience, having sex for money was far better than the long, long list of low-paid, exploitative, going-nowhere jobs I had as a student. I worked briefly as a charity mugger, which was more depressing. I worked in a call center, being shouted at and hung up on by literally thousands of people. I was taken advantage of and underpaid in countless retail jobs and several research ones. Never once did I experience in sex work the dehumanization that I experienced daily in those other jobs (and often for far less pay). And my experience is far from unique.

Most long-term career sex workers don't hate their jobs. But the ones who do deserve labor rights, privacy, and to work in safety. Being vulnerable means their place at the table when discussing these issues should be bigger – not spoken over, spoken for, and ignored.

Anti-trafficking results in wild goose chases. Laws that prosecute the people they're meant to help. Resources directed at a minority of victims, with more and more trafficked workers entering the non-sex labor market every day, invisible to sex trafficking charities.

As the dominoes started to fall, the narrative by anti trafficking orgs shifted: they were simply illustrating what other people went through, the hidden stories of other, nameless, people. Of course there was no proof any of this was happening, because it was all underground. A "hidden crime." If you didn't believe that trafficking was a problem because there was no evidence, that was your problem – not theirs.

Lurid tales of sex abuse have grown so prevalent that the fanatical claims of the alt-right "Pizzagate" conspiracy, which claimed Hillary Clinton was overseeing a child sex ring in nonexistent tunnels beneath a random restaurant in Washington DC, were taken seriously to the point where someone turned up at the pizza place making armed threats. And yet that dangerous breakdown is not enough to stop the well-funded groups that profit off of generating a worldwide panic from withdrawing their ridiculous claims.

Enforcement of current laws should come before creation of new laws. Trafficking is already illegal. Breaking immigration laws is already illegal. Exploiting another person sexually for one's own gain is already illegal. The public, when asked, tends to agree that ensuring current laws are enforced is better than adding another layer of agencies, laws, and potential problems on top if the ones we already have.

What is needed? Outreach to sex workers, who are the first points of contact for trafficking victims, but don't report for fear of being arrested.

We also need greater understanding of the experiences of people who are trafficked, or are labelled as trafficked. Not all see themselves in that way. As a result, a lot of the proposed solutions on offer are not relevant to their experiences. As someone who, by the way trafficking is counted, is supposedly 'trafficked,' it feels like the diverse voices of migrants are ignored. Instead others elect to speak for us. Who does this benefit? Only the ones getting paid for keeping the panic alive.

CHAPTER 7

Anti-intellectualism has been a constant thread winding its way through our political and cultural life, nurtured by the false notion that democracy means that 'my ignorance is just as good as your knowledge.'

Isaac Asimov

In the summer of 2016 I was invited to give evidence to the UK Parliament's home affairs select committee, who had been asked by the Home Office to look into prostitution.

Perhaps 'invited' was the wrong word. I was in the middle of a book tour at the time, and the date – which could not be moved – was incredibly inconvenient, given that testimony would have to be supplied in person in London, while I was then touring the Highlands of Scotland. However it soon became clear that this was not a polite ask; this was an order to appear.

I was not looking forward to it. I had already given a written response to the committee's consultation document, a document which was largely informed by, and parroted the false claims of, the prohibition movement that seeks to bring the 'Swedish Model' of prosecuting sex workers to the UK. All of the briefing in advance of the day was full of one-sided claims, confidently stated, backed up with no evidence. It was clear they had asked me not because I was the best or even the most qualified respondent, but because I was in a small way, famous in Britain. They wanted a well-known hooker to kick around.

On the day I met quickly in the bathroom with the other invited guest: activist and media personality Paris Lees. We agreed we had been set up, that we were called there for 'star power' and to get headlines. So we went in there angry. We went, as they say where I come from, loaded for bear. It's fair to say the Members of Parliament? Had no idea what they were in for.

Members present: Keith Vaz (Chair); James Berry; Mr David Burrowes; Nusrat Ghani; Mr Ranil Jayawardena; Tim Loughton; Stuart C. McDonald; Mr Chuka Umunna; Mr David Winnick

Questions 144–193

Witness[es]: **Paris Lees**, journalist, presenter and equality campaigner, and **Dr Brooke Magnanti**, research scientist, blogger and writer, gave evidence.

Q144 Chair: May I welcome our witnesses, Paris Lees and Dr Brooke Magnanti? Thank you very much for coming. This is part of the Select Committee's inquiry into prostitution. It is the first time Parliament has looked at this issue and we are very grateful to both of you for coming to give evidence today.

May I start with you, Paris Lees? The Committee has looked at a number of models other than the model we have in this country. We have looked at Denmark and Sweden and we may look at other countries as well. Do you think that the law on prostitution at the moment in the United Kingdom is satisfactory, or do you think it ought to be changed?

Paris Lees: I think it ought to be changed. Have you looked at New Zealand?

Chair: No, we haven't.

Paris Lees: Okay, well, I think you should look at New Zealand. I don't think that criminalising sex work makes anybody safer. Criminalising the buying of sex work wouldn't have made me safer. I chose to do sex work as a student in Brighton. If it had been illegal for the men who came to see me and paid for my time, that would not have stopped me doing it; it would have just made them more desperate, paranoid and edgy, and it would have made me more desperate and less able to turn away people who were perhaps drunk or hostile. So no. When I felt safest doing sex work, speaking from personal experience, is when I have been working with friends, which under the current laws would make me a criminal, because of brothel keeping. If we want to look at safety of sex workers, then we need to decriminalise aspects of sex work.

Q145 Chair: Thank you. Dr Magnanti, do you agree with that? Do you think that the law is unsatisfactory? It has been around for a very long time. Do you think it needs to be changed? We will come on to what the changes should be, but at the moment do you think that change is needed?

> *Dr Magnanti:* Absolutely. I do think that it needs to be changed. Obviously we have the 1956 Act, which outlawed brothel keeping and also criminalises any two women working together, whether or not somebody is managing or pimping for someone else, if they just happen to be sharing premises. Then of course there is the Street Offences Act 1959, so anybody who is soliciting on the street is also criminalised.
>
> Obviously, in the position that I was in, I was not really doing either of those things, but people that I worked with were in a position where they would have been criminalised. I myself felt that I was in a fairly safe position, just because the exchange of sex for money is not in and of itself currently illegal; it is more the things surrounding it that are currently illegal. Overall, obviously I come from a reasonably privileged and safe background compared to some people who end up in very chaotic and desperate situations, but don't they deserve to feel as safe doing the work and to feel as able to go to the authorities if they feel threatened as I felt?

Q146 Chair: Both of you have been very open about the fact that you were sex workers at some stage in your lives. Do you think that this could be misunderstood by younger girls, in particular, although of course it could be girls or boys. Do you think that people might see this as something of a career? Did you see it as a career, Paris Lees? Or did you have to do it because you couldn't afford to pay your way at university?

> *Paris Lees:* Well, what's wrong if younger people do see this as a career? If you don't think there is anything wrong with sex work, why would you worry about influencing whether other people choose to do it or not? Did I see it as a career? I saw it as something that enabled me to get on. Yes, I may have made different choices if I had had different choices, but the reality is that I would not have been able to put myself through university without sex work; I would not have got my degree or been able to establish myself in the media, or have been able to get a public

92

profile for myself to talk about these issues and have a voice. I probably wouldn't be sitting here today had it not been for sex work. It has been a really good thing in my life and it has really helped me. All of the accolades and awards that I have won for who I am today are a direct consequence of my having done sex work.

Q147 Chair: And you have never felt under pressure or that someone was making you do this? You have never felt in any way degraded?

Paris Lees: No. I have never been raped. I was a sex worker. I have not been trafficked.

Q148 Chair: Dr Magnanti, do you see this as a career? Do you see yourself as perhaps a role model for others who might want to follow you?

Dr Magnanti: Perhaps as a role model for people who want to become child health scientists. My situation is as a non-EU migrant. In the period between when I submitted my PhD and when I had my viva, there was zero funding. Of course, being non-EU I had no recourse to public funds. I was in a situation where I could either go home and not attend my viva and therefore not obtain my PhD and not have the science career that I had been working for a decade to get to, or I could do sex work. There were also laws in place at the time that forbad non-EU students from working for more than 15 hours per week, and also forbade any employers from employing us where there was any qualified EU applicant. I was basically between a rock and a hard place.

Q149 Chair: So you had to do it?

Dr Magnanti: I saw it as a stopgap, really, in the way that a lot of students would choose to work behind a bar. If working behind a bar had been an option and if it had paid enough to live in London for the months while I was waiting for my viva, sure, that might have been a valid option for me, but it simply wasn't. I think that the root causes—things like migration policy and the social safety net—really need to be looked at very hard before you start piling new laws on top of that.

Q150   Chair: Paris Lees, what about vulnerable women? You must have met some. I can't believe that in your life as a sex worker you did not meet some young women or men who had been forced to do this because they had been trafficked and were the subject of criminal gangs who made them do this. I cannot believe that everyone decided to pursue the career in the way that you have done.

> *Paris Lees:* Well I can't believe that I am speaking to seven middle-aged men in suits who are telling me that this is violence against women. That completely overlooks the fact that guys and transgender people do this as well. To characterise this as exploitation of women is completely ridiculous. If there is exploitation, that is already illegal. No, I have not met anybody like that. I have friends who I have done it with—friends who I used to work with. A friend of mine who did it did not encourage me to do it, but I saw she was doing all right and she had money. These were not screwed up people. Sure, I am from a very poor area—Nottingham, which is one of the poorest areas of the country according to a report I read in 2013, I think. Yes, people do have to make tough choices, but guess what? My grandad had to work down a coal mine. Sometimes people have to do things that—

Q151   Chair: My question is did you meet anyone who was forced to do this for criminal gain by other people? The only people you have met in your career as a sex worker are people who did it voluntarily, is that right?

> *Paris Lees:* That's right, but you say you cannot believe that. Why is it so incredible? If there are so many of them, surely the evidence will show that. Why don't you speak to these people who have been forced into it, if they are out there?

> *Dr Magnanti:* And go into the question—

Q152   Chair: I will come to you in one second, Dr Magnanti. I put it to you because that is what people have said to us. We have had quite a long inquiry and other women have said that they have been exploited.

> *Paris Lees:* Who?

Q153   Chair: I cannot give you the names and details, but they are on the website.

Paris Lees: It seems to me that you have had some people at this inquiry who have absolutely no business talking about sex work; people whose only qualification seems to be that they write for *The Observer.* With all due respect, James, have you ever been in a position where you felt that you needed to sell your body for sex?

James Berry: No—

Paris Lees: It's a fair question.

Chair: It is but it is not a question—

Paris Lees: I think he wants to answer.

Chair: He is not in a position to answer. Ms Lees, when Mr Berry asks you the question you can come to him and put it directly back at him.

Paris Lees: My point is that we are here talking about decisions that are not going to affect any of you or some of the people you have invited to speak here.

Chair: I take your point, and that is why we have invited you to come here.

Dr Magnanti: But it is not going to affect us.

Paris Lees: It is not going to affect us.

Dr Magnanti: This is the thing. We have both left sex work. Of the four sex workers that you have spoken to face to face, three of us are not doing it any more. You have only spoken to one person face to face who is actually currently a sex worker.

Who are the people who should have been asked to be at this table instead of us today? The current sex workers—people from Sex Worker Open University, from the English Collective of Prostitutes, from SCOT-PEP. But they weren't asked because me and Paris, we come with great big media platforms; we come and we bring attention. We are the merkin for these proceedings, so you can tick a box and say, "We spoke to some ex-sex workers." I retired in 2004. I can tell you everything about what was happening in 2003 and 2004. What is going to happen in the laws going forward does not affect me. You need to speak with the biggest stakeholders—those who are the current sex workers and the organisations representing them.

Q154 Chair: We have done. Not all the witnesses whom we've spoken to want to speak in public. When we went to Denmark and Sweden and spoke to workers out there, they were not prepared to—

Dr Magnanti: That isn't what I was given to understand.

Chair: Well, I'm telling you how we conduct our inquiries. If people come forward and ask to give evidence, we obviously would like them to come. They can also give written evidence; they do not all have to give oral evidence. We want to understand this problem of decriminalisation and that is why we have invited you.

Dr Magnanti: Do you think of decriminalisation as a problem?

Chair: No, I think the whole issue causes a lot of controversy. That is why it is important that we look at it.

Dr Magnanti: It causes controversy, but do you think it is ipso facto a problem?

Paris Lees: Controversy isn't a problem in and of itself. Can we identify what the actual problem is?

Q155 Chair: Indeed. That is one of the points that we hope to discover during this inquiry. I have a final question for you. It concerns those who advertise on websites like Sugar Babies, those who are still at school and university—you described how you were in the same position and felt you had to do it. Do you think there should be better regulation of websites that are used in this way or are you happy with the law as it stands?

Paris Lees: I don't really know much about the law about websites but I think there should be better regulation full stop. I don't think that making something underground makes people safer. I am not sure. What is the problem that you want to solve? Do you want to discourage people from doing sex work? If so, I would ask why—why do you want to discourage people from doing that? It just makes no sense to me. I don't know what this inquiry wants to achieve. It is looking at how to end sex work. My question is: why do you want to end sex work?

Chair: Let us turn to Mr Burrowes, who originally suggested this inquiry, which has been very interesting for the Committee. Parliament has never looked at the law on prostitution before.

Q156 Mr Burrowes: First of all, in the context of the Swedish model, they make the case in principle in relation to violence against women and this being a gender issue, as you talked about, but it is not alone. We have heard evidence from prosecuting authorities. The Crown Prosecution Service has written in its documents that prostitution is a form of violence against women. We are not necessarily looking at our views; we are just interrogating the views that are coming across. Do you see any examples at all of prostitution being about violence against women, or anything to do with coercion?

> *Paris Lees:* Violence against women is already illegal, and trafficking is already illegal. You may as well have a Select Committee on whether or not we criminalise people who pay for cleaners because you object to slavery. With the greatest respect, may I ask you if you have ever been in a position where you felt that you needed to sell your body for sex?

Mr Burrowes: I am asking the questions.

> *Paris Lees:* You're asking the questions. Okay, well, I'm going to take a wild guess and say that you haven't. You are making decisions—

Mr Burrowes: I am just asking a question.

> *Paris Lees:* What is your interest? What do you know about it?

Mr Burrowes: I'm asking the questions.

> *Dr Magnanti:* But you work for us.

Mr Burrowes: No, I don't.

> *Dr Magnanti:* Do you not? I'm sorry, what pays your wages?

Mr Burrowes: My constituents are my bosses, not you.

Dr Magnanti: Who are your bosses?

Mr Burrowes: You are here to answer questions. You were invited to answer questions. If you don't want to, you don't need to be here.

Dr Magnanti: I am, but I also think that you have a responsibility to us, because it was very clear to me, from the questions that I was briefed on and that I was going to be answering that I was going to be asked about things that bore absolutely no relationship to the written evidence that I submitted. I was going to be asked how I felt about eastern Europeans, as if I were an eastern European. It really does seem to me that we have legitimate questions to ask about what this Committee is doing.

Q157 Mr Burrowes: In your written evidence, you make reference to Amnesty International and their views in relation to full decriminalisation. They advocate it for sex work that does not involve coercion, exploitation or abuse. On the back of that part of your submission, I ask the question: do you see any—

Dr Magnanti: But I am not here as a representative of Amnesty International. Should you not have asked one of them?

Q158 Mr Burrowes: No, I am referring to your submission in relation to—

Dr Magnanti: So because I have made reference to Amnesty International, I am responsible for answering for their policy?

Q159 Mr Burrowes: You can ask the questions around my questions. I am asking you a direct question and you can answer it or not. Do you see any sex work as involving coercion, exploitation or abuse?

Dr Magnanti: No.

Paris Lees: By definition, it is not sex work if it involves coercion or abuse.

Dr Magnanti: Exactly.

Q160 Mr Burrowes: Do you see any evidence of entry into sex work being an issue that involves people under the age of 18?

Dr Magnanti: Statistically speaking—

Paris Lees: Don't bother with statistics and facts and things like that. They don't want their heads muddled.

Chair: Order, Ms Lees. If Dr Magnanti has some statistics that she wishes to share with the Committee, we would be very happy to hear them.

Dr Magnanti: As a quick summary, just as an overview: I looked at these worldwide, country by country, and the available evidence—obviously for countries such as the UK in western Europe, it is very slightly higher than it is for the rest of the world. In the UK, according to Church et al, the mean is 23 years of age for entry for indoor workers—people such as myself and Paris—and 20 for outdoor. Ward finds that the mean is 24. Jeal and Salisbury find that it is 23.

Over in Ireland, they went with ranges rather than exact numbers. The most common answer, over 50%, was ages 18 to 24. That is five times what it was for the under-18s. In Northern Ireland, 18 to 21 was the range. In Australia, Roxburgh et al gave it as 21. In Switzerland, Brossier gives it as 24. In Canada, O'Doherty gives it as 21, and Goldenberg as 20. In New Zealand, Abel says ages 18 to 21 are the most common answers, and almost—nearly always—50% or higher, for when people first enter sex work.

I was 27. If you look at the websites, of course if you go online they subtract ages. I was advertised as being 23, so I had to pretend to be almost five years younger than I was. That is very common. If you are just looking at the websites as a source for who the people are in sex work, of course they are exaggerations. I know a sex worker who, on the internet, is forever 39, but she is really 43.

Q161 Mr Burrowes: We are looking at our current criminal law and where it needs to be changed. One part of it is that, if you are under 18, prostitution is effectively classified as exploitation. Do you agree with that?

Dr Magnanti: As Paris rightly pointed out, if people are coerced, if they are trafficked or if they are under age, we already have adequate laws to cover that. We don't need to qualify sex work, on the whole, as being abuse against those people, because they are already covered by laws about sexual exploitation, sexual abuse and rape.

Q162 James Berry: The answer to your question, Ms Lees, is no, as you would expect. I have not reached any conclusion about whether the law is right or wrong. What we are trying to do is to explore whether the law is right or wrong—*[Interruption.]* Let me finish, please. If any changes need to be made to the law, Parliament is the only place that is going to do that. Dr Magnanti suggested a sensible change about the brothel keeping issue, because not allowing two women to work in the same room can lead to risk. That change is not going to be made unless this Committee makes a recommendation and the Government accepts it, which is why we are holding this inquiry and why your evidence will be really helpful if you answer the questions. I know that you have criticised who we have heard so far in this inquiry, but we will be hearing from other people. We have recently gone to Sweden and Denmark, and we have spoken to a large number of charities. The evidence that they gave is slightly different from what you said. The evidence that they gave was that, in their experience, the large majority of women involved in prostitution are involved against their will and do not have a particularly pleasant experience, but they accept that a small proportion of women involved in prostitution—

Dr Magnanti: But you didn't speak to—

James Berry: Just let me finish, please. They accept that a small proportion of women involved in prostitution do so voluntarily and have no problem with it, and both of you are included in that. Of course, all laws must have a purpose behind them. As you know, we have heard from witnesses, whose views differ from yours and who are very trenchant about what the purpose of the law should be. Do you think that the purpose of the law should be to reduce the overall amount of sex work that takes place, or to protect, so far as possible, women who choose to go into sex work?

Dr Magnanti: I have a three-part answer. First, my understanding of your visit to Sweden is that you did not speak to anybody, for example, Pye Jakobsson of the Rose Alliance, who represents a sex worker-led organisation. Rather, you spoke to charities that support the sex buyer laws that currently exist.

James Berry: They didn't, actually.

Dr Magnanti: Part of the problem with the statistics that are currently being produced by Sweden is that they don't have any statistics from before the law came into effect, so they make all kinds of claims about how much they have reduced street prostitution and how the people in prostitution feel about it, but in fact they were not polling any sex workers to get a before and after.

The "doctor" part of my name deals on a daily basis with population statistics, and there are a lot of trash population statistics that get bandied about, especially when we talk about places like Sweden and other countries that have either instituted the full sex buyer ban or portions thereof, such as Northern Ireland. They have no basis for comparison, and they have no baseline, so I would be very, very sceptical of anything they are producing. When you look at the statistics worldwide, and when you look at the countries that are most affected by trafficking, we are talking about countries such as India and Cambodia, which unsurprisingly also have very strong sex worker-led organisations. The percentage of people who are actively trafficked is comfortably under 5%. I agree with what all of you are thinking right now, which is that even one is too many. That is absolutely the case, which is why you need input from sex worker-led organisations, which are best placed to be able to identify the needs for finding out where the abuses are happening.

Q163   James Berry: Okay, but would you mind just answering the question? I would really like to get both your answers. Do you think that the aim of the law should be to reduce the overall amount of sex work that takes place or to protect women who choose to undertake it?

Dr Magnanti: I do not really think that should be in there, because it is a very unpredictable thing. For example, when I became a sex worker I was paying university fees of £10,000-plus a year and the associated costs. That was not the case for home and EU students at the time. Obviously, that has changed, so there has been an influx of student sex workers since then. We need to look at the root causes, at what are the push factors rather than the pull factors. These are things that are very much outside of a very focused law that only deals with, "We need to decrease sex workers".

Q164 James Berry: Ms Lees, what is your view on what the purpose of the law that we have should be?

Paris Lees: I would like to respond to your original comment first. It is great that you have an open mind and I really respect that, but I think I was raising a legitimate objection to the fact that sex work is described as violence against women in the literature around this Committee. That is setting out a moral position. I know a lot of sex workers. I have five or six friends back in Nottingham who are sex workers. Three of them are guys. I am transgender, I know lots of people in the LGBT community, I know lots of gay guys who escort, so it just seems bizarre to me that we are legislating in a way that is going to affect those people and describing it as a women-only issue. This is annoying because Harriet Harman described sex work as abuse against women. I was not abused. Were you abused?

Dr Magnanti: No.

Paris Lees: I questioned her about this on Twitter and she said, "Oh, that's just what I think". You can't tell me that I've been abused. This stuff really matters. Should we find ways to make it happen less? Good luck with that. No, I don't think you are going to stop people.

Q165 James Berry: Do you then think that the purpose of the law should be to protect women, as far as possible, who choose to be prostitutes?

Paris Lees: Absolutely. Let's say you've got a client who is going to see an escort, maybe in a brothel or on the internet. They think that the person seems a little edgy, doesn't seem very happy and they suspect that they may have been trafficked. What client is going to go to the police and raise their concerns if they know that they are going to be outing themselves as a criminal? How does that make sex workers safer?

Q166 James Berry: That is a good point. Finally, what, specifically, would you change about the law as it stands now? We have already heard the issue about two prostitutes working in the same building, which is a good point. Is there anything else, apart from that, that you would change about the existing law?

Paris Lees: There are two things. I cannot claim to know the law inside-out; I have come here today to talk about my personal experiences as a former sex worker, but, as I say, of course, you are safer if you are working with somebody. I lived in Brighton about five or six years ago, I was at university there, and there was a sex worker called Andrea Waddell who was murdered. She worked in a flat on her own. I cannot help but wonder if that wouldn't have happened if she had been in a house with other people. This is the reality: you are not safe on your own.

What are you going to do if a client turns violent on you? It has never happened to me, but, of course, you are safer when you are with other people. So I think that this brothel-keeping nonsense needs to go and people need to be safer. Labour, the party that is supposed to stand up for marginalised people and for workers, should actually be advocating for this and allowing sex workers to come together to work in collectives where they feel empowered and safe and not that they are going to be criminalised. That is the first thing.

Secondly, I think it is complete madness to say, "Oh, well, we'll end demand". It just doesn't work, you're not going to stop it. As long as you've got people and a financial system in which people use money, you are going to have people who want to pay for sex.

Chair: Thank you.

James Berry: Thank you for your very trenchantly expressed views. We should have had you in when we had the lady from UK Feminista, who you obviously disagree with. It would have been good if we had had you together.

Dr Magnanti: If I can make a very quick addendum, while we are in a spirit of suggestions, the other thing I would suggest, which has worked out very well in the state of Louisiana in the United States, is wiping the criminal record of people who have been previously convicted for soliciting or brothel keeping. If you really want people to get on with their lives, they should be able to go and apply for jobs, especially if you consider these people to be victims. We can disagree on that point or not, but if you consider that they are victims and that their lives should be improved, people going about with criminal records for having been soliciting on the streets or having been working with a maid in a walk-up is unacceptable.

Paris Lees: Hear, hear.

Q167 Chair: Just to clarify, Ms Lees, the reference to violence against women was in a series of questions that the Committee asked in our press release. It was not the view of the Committee. The Committee will decide its views on this at the end of the inquiry, after we have taken all the evidence. Just to be clear, it was in a press release.

I am not sure that we can describe Mr Jayawardena as middle-aged.

Paris Lees: My apologies.

Chair: I think so—an apology is due.

Paris Lees: Listen: your sex work age would be considerably lower.

Q168 Mr Jayawardena: If I may ask you about some international comparisons, around the world, countries have adopted various approaches towards prostitution. Which model would you prefer to see replicated in the United Kingdom? It does not have to be exactly either of these systems, but a legalised regulated system, such as is the case in Germany and the Netherlands, or a fully decriminalised system, such as the system in New Zealand?

Paris Lees: I would like to see what has happened in New Zealand. I have never been there or spoken to sex workers there, but they seem to be more able to report crime over there.

Dr Magnanti: Friends of mine have worked in New Zealand and also in New South Wales in Australia, which has a very similar system.

Q169 Mr Jayawardena: So you both agree that the fully decriminalised approach would be better? I have another question, then. There are lots of statistics that any of us could look at. Since the European, or Nordic model, if I can call it that, was adopted by Sweden

16 years ago, not a single prostitute has been murdered by a client. That is a legalised, regulated system. In New Zealand, by contrast, with half the population of Sweden, they have lost several prostitutes to murders; so I am struggling with how a fully decriminalised system is safer for prostitutes.

Dr Magnanti: On the one hand, you are comparing countries that have very different laws with regards to walking around armed, so that is something we can put to the side. But in terms of referring to dead bodies—that very emotive subject—what we have in Sweden is a system that absolutely depersonalises sex workers, to the point where a sex work activist was murdered by her ex-husband. That happened at a visitation. Her children had been taken away from her; he was known to be abusive to her, but full custody was given to him. She was prevented from seeing her own children for years. The first time that she was allowed access to those children, her known to be abusive, known to be violent, ex-husband stabbed her to death in front of their own children. He was enabled by a system in Sweden that calls wanting to be a sex worker a pathology. Technically, by the laws on their books, they don't criminalise it, but the way they treat sex workers is as if we are children; as if we should be wards of the state, with no ability to make our own decisions. That was something that really struck at the heart of sex work advocacy, because decriminalisation is not an end goal; it is a first step. Decriminalisation is simply baseline, the starting line. As with any kind of work, anything that is decriminalised—selling alcohol, for example—we still have regulations that come into play about zoning, about where and when things are allowed to happen. Don't think of decriminalisation, don't think that anybody is advocating it as a free-for-all. It is actually a first step, which is then followed up.

Going back to the second part of your question, it was found that sex work was highly stigmatised in New Zealand. Absolutely, there is still violence, but it is improving. People feel that the stigma is dying off; people feel that the individual instances of violence against sex workers are going down. It is not just a, "Make a law, snap your fingers and everything is going to be okay" kind of moment. You have to put it into the greater context of each society that these kinds of laws are enacted in.

Q170 Mr Jayawardena: That is very helpful. We have heard from witnesses on a previous panel that the sex bylaw has reduced overall levels of prostitution in Sweden by about half. Do you recognise that figure, and has the criminalisation of purchase ended the sale of sex or has it simply changed the ways in which it is sold?

> *Dr Magnanti:* I recognise the figure because it gets repeated a lot, but, again, going back to what I was saying to Mr Berry earlier, Sweden did not have a baseline measure of where it was at. They say it has gone down 50%, but they don't have a starting amount. Compared with what? It is absolute guesswork. Also, when they use that figure they are not talking about all sex work; they are talking about visible, on-the-street sex work— what we would consider to be the cliché of the woman leaning into the car. There is other evidence that shows that indoor sex work has gone up, and there is even more evidence that has shown that trafficking is going up in Sweden because the people who are going into sex work feel unsafe. If they cannot turn to the police and they cannot turn to the state, who do they go to? They go to criminals. That is why decriminalisation is needed.

Q171 Mr Jayawardena: On that basis, a proposed change from the status quo in the United Kingdom to something like the Swedish model is not helpful.

> *Dr Magnanti:* I don't think it would be, no.

Q172 Mr Jayawardena: May I pursue one question with Dr Magnanti directly? You have long advocated decriminalisation—

> *Dr Magnanti:* I haven't always, actually.

Mr Jayawardena: But you've long advocated it.

> *Dr Magnanti:* Since around 2012.

Chair: That's quite long.

> *Dr Magnanti:* There was a much longer period of not.

Mr Jayawardena: A week is a long time in politics.

> *Dr Magnanti:* Indeed.

Q173   Mr Jayawardena: Many critics of yours would argue that your time as a high-class escort earning hundreds of pounds bears little resemblance to the experience of many sex workers working on the street and in brothels who may struggle with addictions and the threat of violence. Do you accept that your positive experiences as a sex worker may be unrepresentative of many out there?

Dr Magnanti: Absolutely. There is no one sex worker who is representative of all sex work. As I said to Mr Vaz earlier, doesn't everybody in sex work deserve to feel as safe and secure in their work as I did? Don't we owe it to the people who are out on the street to think that when they are in danger they can pick up the phone and speak to the police or social services? They don't currently feel that way, which is why we have things such as National Ugly Mugs, where sex workers are sharing information between themselves because they do not feel safe enough going to the police. By and large, where both sides of sex work are criminalised—I am talking about places such as the United States, which has, by any standards, an incredibly repressive model that, let's be fair, I don't think anybody wants to implement—the most frequent rapists of sex workers are actually the police.

Q174   Mr Jayawardena: But you're not suggesting that that is the case here.

Dr Magnanti: No, I'm not, but when you say you are looking at models worldwide, that puts it in context.

Q175   Mr Jayawardena: So what you are saying is that we need to ensure that, when crimes are committed, people feel able to report them to the police.

Dr Magnanti: Absolutely.

Q176   Mr Jayawardena: Would you agree with that as well, Ms Lees?

Paris Lees: I would agree with that. In answer to your original question, have we found a country with a model where they have completely got rid of sex work? I don't think we have, have we? Ultimately, we need to accept that people are going to do this on some level. Again, I can speak only from my personal experiences. I once had to call the police about a client. He was drunk and became very hostile and aggressive and I didn't feel safe. I called the police and they were really good. They turned up and there were loads of them—five or six. I felt able to do that because although there is a lot of confusion about just what is and isn't illegal, I thought that I was okay. It wouldn't have made me safer if buying sex work had been criminalised. As regards Brooke's experiences being quite privileged, they probably are compared with some people's.

Dr Magnanti: I'm not denying that.

Paris Lees: I've done the high-class thing and I've also been on the street before. I have seen lots of different aspects of sex work. The parts of town I was in were the really dodgy, rough parts of town because that's where you go—that's where people go missing.

Q177 **Chair:** But isn't that the problem: the difficulty of legislating when you have, at least, a two-tier system? You can have someone earning a lot of money per night, some £1,200—I think Helen Wood was an example—and this morning, when I was talking to BBC Radio Leeds, there was an 18-year-old eastern European girl who was earning £5 a night. It is difficult for Parliament to legislate to cover both those examples, isn't it?

Dr Magnanti: I completely agree with you. Part of the problem is that you are talking about extremes. Good laws are never made out of the extremes. You have the 10% at the top end like me, who are advertised on very glossy websites, and it is all very lah-di-dah. Then you have the 10% at the bottom who are in absolutely desperate circumstances. We are missing what is going on in the middle and the variety, which Paris is possibly more representative of than I am, of what is going on in the middle. Those are the people who need money for the same reasons as anybody who goes to work in a supermarket or in a night-time bakery, baking things for the supermarket. So, really, when we look at the Helen Woods or the Belle de Jours of the world, we say, "Well, there's her and there's everyone else". Assuming that a two-tier system exists is to overlook the vast middle. More than 80% of sex workers are in the middle.

Chair: That is a very important point.

Q178   Mr Winnick: I have listened very carefully to the evidence you have given, as all my colleagues have. Recognising the exceptions, would it not be correct to say that, to a very large extent, those who come into prostitution in the main have problems that perhaps other women or other males do not have, such as family problems or abuse, and that they go into prostitution first and foremost for economic reasons? They do not particularly want to be sex workers, but it is a means of getting a livelihood that, otherwise, they would not be able to obtain. Would that be a realistic picture?

Dr Magnanti: But isn't that most jobs?

Paris Lees: Don't most people work for economic reasons?

Mr Winnick: Yes.

Paris Lees: I worked in a call centre when I was 16, selling dodgy timeshares for economic reasons. I didn't like it but I was paid for it. That is the nature of work, surely. Yes, people do it because they need to do it but if we are really concerned about people from marginalised backgrounds, such as me, we need to look at austerity, the dismantling of the welfare state, and people having safe routes to get here from other countries if they are fleeing and they are desperate.

Q179   Mr Winnick: That more or less confirms what I was saying. They are marginalised because of various failures, which you have just mentioned. Therefore, they are somewhat different from others. Most people, unless they have a private income or expect to inherit a great deal of money or a combination of both, have no alternative but to find jobs. The picture being painted may be totally wrong—we are learning—but is it not possible that there is a difference between the vast majority of those who take up employment as there is no alternative, and those who take up work as sex workers?

Dr Magnanti: Are you asking whether there is some kind of—

Mr Winnick: Special factors, yes.

Dr Magnanti: Something that makes me as an individual different?

Mr Winnick: Economic factors.

Dr Magnanti: Well, going back to reinforce what Paris was saying, the economic factors vary. It could be a non-EU migrant such as me, who has absolutely no recourse to other funds, and the employment that is available—where it is available—would not have paid the bills, or we could be talking about people who go from being marginally in the black to in the red because of the bedroom tax and because of the failure of the social safety net to catch them, which, unfortunately, is happening to an increasing level.

Mr Winnick: As a Labour Member, I would not disagree with that.

Paris Lees: David, I would really like to answer your question. I can only speak about my own personal experience. As I say, I am from a really rough estate in Nottingham. I am transgender and, like many transgender people, I experienced family rejection as a teenager when I came out at 18. I had applied to go to university and I was the first person in my family to go to university. My dad is a doorman and my mum worked in a pub when I was growing up. She has a better job now. I was not getting proper support on the NHS, like many transgender people. I did not feel safe living in student halls because I had mental health issues at the time. I was suffering from depression and things. I did not have a nice middle class family to bankroll me. I had to pay for laser hair removal, which is not available on the NHS in any case. I needed to work and I had problems leaving the house.

Sex work helped me. The point is that I would have remained marginalised if it hadn't been for sex work: I wouldn't have my degree, I wouldn't have been able to establish a career. I know people from my home town who have nothing. We weren't ever raised to believe we would have anything. A few years ago, I heard someone speaking at the Fabian Society, which I'm sure you're all aware of. It was a middle-class commentator; she was saying, "We were told that if we worked hard, these were the things we could have—we could have a house, we could have stability." I was never told that. I thought the best I could hope for was a job in the pub and maybe buying my own council house. Sex work has allowed me to find a way out of that. It is the reason why I am privileged now and not marginalised.

I'm not allowed to ask you questions, but I guess my question would be "What would you have done for me?" How else could I have got out of being marginalised? What are the alternatives?

Q180 Mr Winnick: There is one other aspect, which is different. You say, "Other people take employment of various kinds—what's the difference with being a sex worker?". I suppose the concern is over violence: sex workers, particularly women, are more likely to be subject to violence, and sometimes murderous violence, than other employees. Isn't that a factor that this Committee should take into account?

Paris Lees: Absolutely. The other difference from sex work—again, I don't speak for all sex workers—is that when I worked in a call centre, I think it was £5 a hour, but when I was doing all right, it was £200 or £300. If you need money, you're going to go for the one that pays more, aren't you? If it's slightly more dangerous, I repeat that that's because it's been pushed underground; it's made seedy. When I had to call the police that time—let's say it had been illegal for me to be selling sex. First, I probably wouldn't have called the police. Secondly, if I had, let's say one of them wanted to coerce me into doing something, because they knew I wouldn't object because they've got this thing hanging over me. If it's dangerous, let's look at ways to make it safer. Surely the best way to do that is to allow people to come together as collectives, to make it all above board and out in the open—taxed, even, if you like.

Dr Magnanti: I paid taxes.

Paris Lees: Did you?

Dr Magnanti: I had an accountant and all.

Chair: Excellent. Thank you very much. I am sure Mr Osborne will be pleased about that.

We need to move on; we have other questions and we need to end the session. This is just to let you know that Mr McDonald only turned 38 last week. Stuart McDonald.

Paris Lees: A spring chicken!

Q181   Stuart C. McDonald: A question that follows what you said about decriminalisation not being the end goal, Dr Magnanti, what would you describe as the end goal? Is it to see prostitution on a par with other career choices and as legitimate as other career choices, or would you not go as far as that? If you would go as far as that, how would you make that happen? What else needs to happen?

Dr Magnanti: How would I do it? Well, I'd wave my magic wand—

Stuart C. McDonald: First of all, is that what you're aiming for, ultimately?

Dr Magnanti: I think that's a fair interpretation of what I said. First, decriminalisation: getting rid of the penalties against sex workers, the brothel-keeping penalties that penalise them for working together or even sharing premises, the laws that penalise them for solicitation. Then if you look further, for example at what's been done in New South Wales and Australia, you have different types of sex workers. You have people who are freelancers, if you will—escorts working out of their home or doing outcalls to people's hotels. You also have licensed brothels.

There could be some kind of licensing in place. For example, the analogy I drew was with the decriminalisation of alcohol. I'm American originally, so this is a big deal for us: the lessons of prohibition loom extremely large. After prohibition was overturned, it wasn't just a free-for-all—not just anybody can make and sell alcohol, but the drinking of it was legalised. Then, of course, you see where there are various laws put in place that kind of nudge things into a safer place.

The bottom line really has to be overall safety. We have to prioritise the safety of the people doing the work, wherever they happen to be doing it, whether it is on their own premises, whether it is a shared premises with other sex workers, or whether it is in a brothel, on camera or what-have-you.

Q182   Stuart C. McDonald: Ms Lees, is the end goal to see prostitution as legitimate a career option as anything else? If so, what—beyond decriminalisation—has to happen to allow that to take place?

Paris Lees: "As legitimate a career option as anything else"—well, that would be nice, wouldn't it? I think there is always going to be a moral position on sex work, just because it involves sex and that is what human morals, morality, laws and social customs have traditionally concerned themselves with—what people can and cannot do sexually. I believe in consent; I believe that consenting adults should be allowed to do what they want with one another and that the state has no business telling them that they can't.

The end point is reducing stigma. The worst part of being a sex worker for me was the social stigma—telling people at university, "This is how I make my money", because I've never been ashamed of what I did. It was a choice that I made, I was an adult and I was happy to do it, and they would go, "Oh, you should respect yourself more", and they'd shame me and they would judge me and they would try to dissuade me from doing it. What this boils down to is people just don't want you to do it and they want to try to find ways to stop you from doing it, and that is what I object to.

Q183   Stuart C. McDonald: Following on from that, despite what you're saying about trying to make it seem as legitimate a career choice as anything else, at times during your evidence sessions both of you have sort of talked about it almost as if it was a matter of last resort—there was no option for you other than to work as prostitutes. Is that because of the stigma that you have just referred to? It's not because you have a particular view that that is a less desirable option?

Dr Magnanti: The stigma is absolutely part of that; it is because you know how people will react. It's not that I felt any qualms particularly; if we're being quite frank, I was hardly a virgin at the age of 27 and never married. That didn't trouble me. It was more my concern about how the people around me would react and whether there would be blowback onto my science career once people knew.

Paris Lees: I think that we're getting a little bit confused. Just because you feel like you have to do something doesn't mean you've been coerced into doing it. I was in a little bit of debt before Christmas and I was offered my first acting gig earlier this year. It was up in Manchester and I didn't really know if I wanted to do it, and it wasn't convenient for me to do it, but I kind of felt like I had to, because I get a couple of grand for it.

What does it mean? My mum has to get up and go to work. If you're getting paid to do something and you're making a choice—a lot of people don't want to work. That's the nature of work—that's why you get paid for it—but it doesn't mean that you've been forced. You choose the work that you want to be paid for, and for me, at that time in my life, it was sex work.

Q184   Stuart C. McDonald: Sure—absolutely—although I think you said that if you'd had other options, you might have done something else. What you are saying is that it is not so much about banning any particular option; it is about making those options more realistic and available.

Paris Lees: Guess what? If I could be Madonna's stylist and pick out clothes all day, in an ideal world that's what I would choose, but I choose to write things because that is how I make money at the moment.

Dr Magnanti: Same.

Paris Lees: And I choose to go on television, and I choose to do things like that, and I get paid for it, but if I had better options I might stop doing it.

Q185   Stuart C. McDonald: One last question, if I may, to clear something up. A couple of times you referred to problems that prostitutes might have in contacting the police or other services, but if we decriminalised the selling of sex and criminalised the purchase of sex why would prostitutes have a difficulty in contacting the police?

Dr Magnanti: Because they know they become the evidence, and this has been the case in countries like Sweden, where the sex worker contacts the police and she may not be arrested for selling sex but she has identified herself as a sex worker to the police, so they are instantly suspicious: "We need to see your papers; we need to see whether you are legal to be here; we need to examine your premises," and all the rest of it. She may also be coerced by the police into giving evidence against other people. Things that have happened in Sweden include people's phones being bugged and people being thrown out of where they live because their landlords are afraid that they are going to be prosecuted as pimps. Yes, technically the selling of sex is not illegal, but it makes an environment where they fear the reaction of all of the people around them. Those people around them, once they know that they are sex workers, fear being prosecuted by that law.

Paris Lees: I would like to answer the questions.

Chair: Very quickly, because we need to move on to Mr Loughton.

Paris Lees: I have been in the situation before where clients call you up, and maybe your rate is £100 for whatever, and they will say, "Oh, you know, I've only got £80" and whatnot. By criminalising the buying of sex and maybe, yes, dissuading some people from doing it, you have got fewer clients. When you haven't had a client for a few days and you really need some money and your rent is due on Monday you are going to be more willing to accept—and it is about empowering. I think anything that disempowers sex workers is not going to make them feel like they are part of the process. The other thing that I would say is—you know, should we try and dissuade it; would that help? If that group of people want to pay for sex and that group of people want to be paid for sex, why would you even want to reduce it?

Chair: Thank you. Final question, Mr Loughton.

Q186 Tim Loughton: Dr Magnanti, your point about Sweden and prostitutes effectively becoming prosecution witnesses against their own clients is absolutely right, from our visit there.

I think it was President Reagan who said that prostitution was the oldest profession for which no formal qualification was deemed necessary, and politics was the second—so we actually might have quite a lot in common. Can I gently say that I think you may have pre-judged this inquiry to a degree. I do not know what our findings are going to be. For my part, as we have gone on, I am increasingly of the view that decriminalising—having everything above board, so that sex workers have full protection, and concentrating on the real criminals in this, who are those who exploit sex workers—is an increasingly attractive way to go.

I also think you are being slightly selective in the reading of what we have done. If you look at the transcript of our previous witnesses you will see that I and others question seriously the qualification of violence against women, asking how you define men sex workers and others, and that those answers were found lacking, as they were in Sweden. However, as you have said, you are not representative of sex workers. Do you acknowledge that there are people involved in sex work in this country who are effectively trapped in it?

> *Dr Magnanti:* I would not call them sex workers, though, and I think that is where we have a problem of terminology. If somebody is having sex against their will, that's rape, you know.

> *Paris Lees:* I have two things to say. Again—the cleaning analogy. If you are a cleaner, what does that mean, to be trapped? If someone has to clean to make money, does that make that person a slave? No, it doesn't. It just means that that's their job. There's a difference between slaves and cleaners, and there's a difference between sex workers and people who are being forced to have sex against their will and are effectively being raped.

> In response to your comments, I would like to say this: I'm sorry if I seem a little bit prickly, but the fact is that we are all very privileged people in this room. You are so privileged sitting here, and you get to make decisions that affect the lives of people who aren't in this room. We are here talking to you today is because we are also privileged now. It is just very frustrating that people are authoring reports arguing that the purchase of sex should be criminalised when they have never had to make these decisions. So I just find it very frustrating.

Q187 Tim Loughton: I understand. Whether we are privileged or not, we have not yet written a Report. We have made no recommendations, and we have a responsibility to seek and take evidence where we can find it. We have more evidence to take, which I think might fill some of the gaps you have identified.

Going back to your definition of a sex worker, let's take an 18 or 19-year-old girl who is a prostitute on the streets and may have an addiction to drugs or alcohol, and who may be in debt to a pimp because she has been trafficked or manipulated in some way. Is that person not trapped?

Paris Lees: I feel like you are obfuscating the issue.

Tim Loughton: I was quite clear. It was a quite clear, very realistic example.

Paris Lees: Well, okay, let me be clear then. I was in debt before Christmas and I took a job because I needed some money. Lots of people are desperate in this country at the moment and are having to do things to get money. That is not the same as being coerced. People make decisions—unless they are being forced, are locked in a house and don't speak English. I am sure that there probably are people who are being abused in that way and that is a terrible, horrible thing, but I do not think that that is the basis for making laws that affect countless people who are just getting on with it and are happy to do it.

Q188 Tim Loughton: So let's go back to this example. You do not think that there are people in that position who are trapped, who would like to come out of prostitution. You acknowledged that there are some people who have got into prostitution for whatever reasons and would now like to come out of it but cannot, because they see it as the only way they can earn money to feed an addiction or pay a pimp, and they are being manipulated. Is that not a good definition of someone who is trapped and for whom the law might need to change, to help them safely out of prostitution, if that is really what they want?

Paris Lees: I find the example bizarre. There are lots of people who probably feel trapped in their jobs and feel that they cannot leave because they need to work to survive. I did not have a drug problem. It is a very complex issue. Yes, I know people who took drugs on the street, but that was people with drug problems or mental health issues, so you would have to take them on a case-by-case basis. I do not think that plucking a hypothetical situation out of the air helps.

Q189 Tim Loughton: Okay, let me put forward a hypothetical situation that is backed up by statistics, without going into the statistics. Would you acknowledge that it is the case that sex workers disproportionately have a drug or alcohol addiction—

Dr Magnanti: The statistics do not show that.

Tim Loughton: Let me finish. Also, that disproportionately to their peer group they may have a history of being abused as children—

Dr Magnanti: These are not statistics.

Tim Loughton: And disproportionately, against their peer group, they are subject to violence and murder. Of course, we have many examples. That is the difference between being a sex worker and being someone who works in a call centre—

Dr Magnanti: Okay, the first example—

Chair: Dr Magnanti, we just cannot make a record of this if people talk over each other. Have you finished, Mr Loughton?

Tim Loughton: That is why I am trying to differentiate between someone who is a sex worker and someone who chooses to work in a call centre. There is a difference. Can you not acknowledge that?

Paris Lees: Okay, I would like to answer. I read something the other day that said that people who have been abused as children are four times more likely to have plastic surgery as adults. What are you going to do—ban plastic surgery? Yes, LGBT people are more likely to suffer mental issues. People from ethnic minorities are more likely to suffer mental health issues. These are complicated issues. Will you stop people doing things because they come from certain backgrounds?

If people are not able to make decisions for themselves, they are not able to make decisions for themselves, but the reality is that there are a lot of people who have suffered abuse and they are just doing what they need to do to get on. It is confusing the issue to confuse it with drug addiction.

Q190 Tim Loughton: So you do not think that sex workers are proportionately more vulnerable in any of those terms than their peer group?

Paris Lees: As I have said several times, the ways in which they are vulnerable and the ways in which I felt, or was, more vulnerable are due to the way the law criminalises aspects of sex work at the moment.

Tim Loughton: Yes, but you have admitted that you are not representative—

Paris Lees: But you are asking—

Tim Loughton: Perhaps Dr Magnanti, you can—

Paris Lees: No one is representative of all sex workers.

Q191 Tim Loughton: Quite so. Therefore, do you not acknowledge, from an academic basis, that there is a difference; that young women who choose, for whatever reasons, to go into sex work have a different sort of vulnerability, which might lead to more of them being trapped, compared with someone who might be trapped, as you put it, working in a call centre, as you did. I am just trying to get to the basis. Do you not see that these people are more vulnerable, potentially?

Dr Magnanti: Going back to the original questions that you asked Paris, the statistics do not show that sex workers are more likely to have drug abuse problems than their peer groups. No, the statistics do not show that sex workers are more likely to have a background of abuse or mental health problems than their peer groups. As Paris rightly mentioned, when we talk about the peer groups of people who go into sex work, these are people from ethnic minorities, people who are migrants and people who are LGBT. They have these conditions because of the stigma that is attached to them, so you are looking at a much wider cultural phenomenon than sex work itself and at people being driven into sex work as a function of being dispossessed in society as a whole.

So I do not agree with the way that you have set up the question, because I do not think that the statistics support that. I wrote a book several years ago that goes into great detail on this. I will leave behind a copy, which obviously you are welcome to peruse, because I'm sure you don't want me to go into that great detail now. The book is cross-referenced with all the relevant studies, so that you can read the original material for yourself and decide whether you feel that these studies are relevant sources for your inquiry.

Chair: Thank you. Are we done?

Tim Loughton: I think we have to be.

Q192 Chair: There are a number of initiatives which have been started. One of them was put forward by Detective Inspector Kevin Hyland, which we heard about in a previous evidence session. This would involve women from religious orders joining the police at the coalface, on the frontline, to assist the police in rescuing women who had been trafficked into prostitution. Cardinal Nichols, the Archbishop of Westminster, backed the scheme, and said that the presence of these nuns would encourage women to desist from being involved. What do you think?

> *Dr Magnanti:* I'm of mixed Catholic and Jewish heritage. When I was 12 years old—which was years before I even had sex, and years before my first kiss—I was told by a nun that I was going to hell. I cannot imagine anything more offputting than the involvement of the Church, and specifically the Catholic Church.

Q193 Chair: So, no nuns needed?

> *Dr Magnanti:* No nuns required. Look at the situation in Northern Ireland, for example. I know that Catholics are a minority in this country, but I think that there are enough people with a similar enough background of exposure to various offices of the Church that they would be extremely sceptical of any so-called help that it might offer.

Chair: Can I thank both witnesses for coming in? The Committee has listened very carefully to your evidence, Paris Lees and Dr Magnanti. It is very helpful to us in our inquiry. We haven't completed the inquiry, and we are taking evidence from other witnesses. We will certainly look at the suggestions that you have made, because we want the broadest possible number of people to come before us. This is simply because after we have completed our inquiry Parliament probably will not look at this again for many years.

For as long as the Select Committee system has been in operation, we have not looked at prostitution. That is why we are looking at it. I hope that what you have had to say will be of great help to the Committee. What I have heard today has certainly been very helpful. You will be very pleased, Paris Lees, that we have been joined by a woman member of the Committee, so we are no longer all male, as you said.

> *Paris Lees:* Hello.

Nusrat Ghani: Hi, sorry I was late.

Chair: That hopefully will be of good use to you. Thank you both very much for coming. We really appreciate it.

The televised hearing went viral, as much for my and Paris's refusal to accept lies as truth as anything else. It was a stressful day, but also a funny one, in retrospect. We retired to the bar and I vowed never to do anything like that ever again.

To my great surprise when the committee released their recommendations several months later? It turned out they had been listening after all. They reversed their stance on the positions put forward in the original consultation. Now they suggested wiping criminal records of sex workers who had been prosecuted so they could move on with their lives. They acknowledged the need to help sex workers operate in safety, and how sharing premises was part of that.

In short: they started to move away from the propaganda they had been fed – towards true decriminalization.

How did this happen? It is difficult to say for sure. One thing that is certain is that proponents of the Swedish Model were on the phone or barraging the committee members with email daily. Our presence was meant to create headlines that mocked sex workers – instead, it was the politicians who were mocked. With Britain's ruling class dominated by dilettantish PPE graduates of Oxford (and those who aspire to be that way), the presence of people who had a deep and personal command of the information they were trying to skate over shook them. The fact that they not only tried to ignore, but also attempted to belittle, people whose stand was not tied up in ideology but rooted in real life and hard data, was exposed for the country to see. A committee that had supposedly been examining the issue for over a year were revealed to have little depth on the topic beyond a cursory Google search. To not have changed their conclusions as a result would have been foolish.

The reactions in media were interesting. Anti-sex activists, who claim only they have the best interests of women in prostitution at heart, were angry MPs dared suggest sex workers convicted of petty crimes might have their records wiped, the better to exit sex work. It was a telling reaction. Hang on... so Julie Bindel et al. don't want to decriminalize sex workers after all? Well, no – as sex workers have repeatedly said, the Swedish Model is not decrim. And the Swedish Model Army showed their true colors by refusing to support a policy that would have helped the most disadvantaged.

With the new Prime Minister, Theresa May, now running things it is unclear where the committee's recommendations will go or if they will ever be implemented in the UK. But as a document, the final judgment is incredible reading. And that small breakthrough came exactly because sex workers refused to remain unheard.

AFTERWORD

It is not your profession that makes you a good or a bad person, and the work you do does not give you dignity; the dignity comes from you. It is said to be indecent work, but we say, it's not indecent...what is indecent are the conditions I have to work in. Indecent is the fact that the health workers who should provide me with humane and quality care discriminate against me. Indecent is the fact that I pay taxes so that the police can be paid their wages, and they repay me with beatings."

Elena Reynaga, executive secretary of RedTraSex, Latin American sex worker collective

How stories are reported has a huge influence on what people believe and how prominent issues are seen to be. As Charles Darwin said, "Great is the power of steady misrepresentation." That misrepresentation is purposeful from some people, while others simply follow along. In the quest to fill pages and cut costs, few papers devote time to checking stories, and press releases are taken at face value. Media re-reports mistakes long after they have been discredited. Making sure "both sides are represented" gives prejudice the same weight as factual material. Journalists summarize without checking their sources.

The media focus both reflects and influences what new laws are created. As Otto von Bismarck famously said, laws are like sausages — it is best not to see them being made. If this sounds unnecessarily harsh, my summary is based on experience. As a columnist for the UK's right-leaning Telegraph newspaper for two years I saw firsthand how the sausage is made. Primary reporting is underfunded and the newspaper was hemorrhaging staff on a weekly basis, established editors and reporters were being replaced by cheap zero-hours workers who knew little and cost less. I was fed suggested topics three times a week by an editor struggling to keep her job, whose continued employment depended on attracting website traffic and advertisers. Struggling to meet deadlines while remaining true to my beliefs as a writer was difficult to maintain. After a deluge of abuse for daring to write in support of Scottish independence, I finally left. But I was glad for the lessons learned.

We're lucky if reporters read to the end of press releases; studies and data presented in them are almost never confirmed. As a scientist I was taught early the value of original sources. Disciplines like history also place high value on the original source. By comparison almost everything you read in the news media is a summary or an interpretation rushed out to try to catch a topic while it's trending. Being able to read and interpret information for yourself is important – vitally so.

The debacle over trafficking is an example of this. A newspaper covers a politician's letter, which then becomes a source that enters government discussion, the transcript of which itself becomes evidence for another newspaper article. How real data can break into the loop is anyone's guess.

Media are obsessed with promoting a view we would previously have dismissed as Victorian. There are indeed parallels. The end of the 19th century and start of the 20th brought new technologies to add to the dissemination of ideas through mass media (much like the Internet today)... with the predictable horror and blame that brought then, just like now. The political class made some unexpected alliances as a result; again, we see this happening.

Along with the news media, feminism also has a charge to answer. Feminism has joined the anti-sex bandwagon in a big way. Not just by blaming men for inequality between the sexes, but perhaps more profitably and successfully by blaming other women.

Many mainstream feminist critiques gloss over old 'man-hating' attitudes and place blame squarely on other women. Instead of embracing women who challenge convention, the preoccupation is with shooting them down.

Consider Julie Bindel's book which claims its remit is ending violence against women. If that is the case, why is so much of the text given over to attacking sex workers, specifically a large number of women? If as Bindel and her ideological mates claim their aim is to end demand for sex, why do they only ever attack the service providers? People like her want to have it both ways: claiming to save women by monstering them. Demonizing bad women to make more space in the discussion for themselves. And, by extension, more money.

On the one hand, we're told that anyone who believes women and men should have equal rights under the law is a feminist, whether they know it or not. On the other, we are told that one or another group of women are traitors. It's the feminists who have taken up the finger-wagging role of the patriarchy. And they rarely if ever address the reasons people go into sex work, namely, that they need money. The enormous inequalities in our society are exactly reflected in who makes up the majority of sex workers: migrants, trans people, people with addictions and disabilities, people of color, the homeless, the poor.

Because of this, feminism has real problems. Its desire to embrace all women is undermined by its compulsion to demonize a large percentage of them. It speaks by and large for a good-girl, middle-class, white experience of womanhood. It marches in the streets for the right to 'reclaim' the word slut in the popular Slutwalks. It also marches in the streets for the right to belittle and ridicule Playboy Bunnies outside a club in London. Capital-F Feminism is a brand few people identify with, while small-f feminism is still an ideal most people support. It leads to an atmosphere that pushes away more potential allies than it draws in.

Take, for example, this quote by Julie Burchill: 'When the sex war is won prostitutes should be shot as collaborators for their terrible betrayal of all women.' Advocating the murder of large numbers of women is such a great way to win supporters to the cause, no?

The great irony is the people protesting that sex workers' clients consider women disposable also consider the same women disposable. All we are is bodies to prop up their shoddy arguments. They can not see that stripper is a woman. Sex workers are women. The category is big enough to handle us all, from cis women to trans women to those who question their gender and sexuality. It is strong enough to handle all histories, be they Ivy League, topless models, or living on the streets.

The narrative in which women who display sexuality are victims and must be educated or otherwise made to pay, and in which men are uncontrollable predators is echoed in everything from fundamentalist propaganda to horror films. It seems women, regardless of the gaze – be it male or female – are ruined by raucous behavior. Women have sinned, gone wild, been tricked, or internalized the oppressor. Take your pick. No matter which you choose, we all lose.

The more you look at the key players behind the panics, the more you notice odd pairings. A group working closely with the anti-gay, anti-abortion US lobbying group using a female MP as the mouthpiece of their opinions on porn. The well-known feminists signing up to work with far right groups. Celebrities lending star power to issues they don't understand at all.

How can we change this? We can start by being wary of policies being sold to government, not to communities.

Take, for instance, the 'sexualization' myth. This has bypassed the people whose interest is the greatest (families) and gone straight to top-level consultation instead. It's not only that government might not understand the issues at stake; they often have misaligned agendas. Solving a problem is not as valuable to them as winning votes. The kudos for bringing in a new policy can be irresistible. If it all goes wrong, as it often does, the government can move on to the next policy, or blame others for its failure.

The 'Swedish model' of sex work is an example of this. Lots of hype, not a lot of data on whether anything has improved. Columnists like Joan Smith can gush about jumping in to cop cars for ridealongs in Sweden, all while ignoring the fact that sex workers repeatedly confirm that the police are their greatest source of harassment, assault, and rape.

There is an impression when it comes to public policy that any idea, no matter how flimsy, must be rolled out big and now. More consultations, more policies, bigger conferences, more media coverage. The 'sex trafficking' issue is one example. Few ask if the increase in activity is producing results – or even if the problem exists at all.

In the age of social media astroturfing and fake news, there are more accounts of agencies and charities claiming to 'raise awareness' about trafficking than there are actual identified victims. Facebook likes and Twitter RTs make people feel as if they are doing something important, and the spread of misinformation is preferred to the uncomfortable truth.

When in doubt, follow the money. Over and over again the people fronting these campaigns are connected to industries with vested interests, radical right-wing think tanks, or anti-LGBT lobbyists. The deputy editor for the New Statesman previously worked at the Mail and is rumored to have subedited Jan Moir when she wrote a viciously homophobic column about Stephen Gately's death. Arch feminists like Julie Bindel write for staunchly right wing, regressive magazines like the *Spectator* and willingly shares stages with the likes of alt-right figurehead Milo Yiannopoulos.

It's notable that almost all of them – save a few token faces – are white. Poverty, migration, and homelessness are not part of their daily lives. When challenged, columnists like Julie Burchill and Suzanne Moore resort to bragging about all the lobster and champagne their unresearched writing buys them.[cxxxiii] None have experience or education in the field they claim to be 'experts' on. Their puddle-deep analysis is misleading and dangerous.

There's a saying where I come from: you got to dance with the one who brung you. I wonder, when everyone gets to the end of their dance cards, what promises feminists have made and what obligations they'll have to honor.

Until 2009, I would have called myself a feminist without reservation. As I understood it, feminism meant the straightforward notion that women should have the same rights as men. So far, so naïve.

When I wrote books under a pseudonym about my experiences as a sex worker, there was no small amount of grumbling in the press. After I won the Guardian Best British Weblog award in 2003, a number of female contributors to that paper signed a letter vowing that if I was commissioned to write for the paper, they would quit. Yet I continued to believe that if they knew I was real, they would feel differently.

As I saw it, sex work is an issue not unlike abortion access. Many agree they would not like to do it. Many agree it is often a difficult choice made under less-than-ideal circumstances. And yet we can say with confidence that making it safe and legal is better than the alternatives. That harm reduction is the way forward.

It's probably not a surprise to you that I was unprepared for what any fool could have predicted would happen.

What was most maddening about the analysis after I came out as an ex-sex worker who is now a science researcher was the discussion about me as an object and not a person. Not so much by the tabloids I'd feared, as the feminists I'd revered.

It is clear that in some minds, to be a prostitute at all is to be a prostitute only. It's very patronizing. They believe having been a sex worker at any time strips you of any other permissible identity and defines you absolutely. It makes you open to ridicule, regardless of your credentials in any other sphere of life. It even somehow disqualifies you from talking about sex work!

I have been criticized for being too middle class, too well educated, too independent. As if my very existence in sex work was, somehow, unique. Then, when I mentioned in an interview I had once been homeless in the mid 90s? That was used to write me off, too. So which is it – too privileged to understand poverty, or too poor to make a real choice? No one seems to be able to answer.

It is bizarre to read articles by people who've never met me attempting to dissect this or that bit of my life. Some lazy commentators 'blame' me for the existence of other call girls, or whatever new student sex worker is uncovered by the tabloids. As flattering as that is, it is not true. Prostitution is called 'the oldest profession' for a reason.

When the first edition of this book was published in Britain in 2012, it was embargoed before publication day and available to fewer than 20 people to review. Journalists who saw the book signed confidentiality agreements. So it was a great surprise to wake up on the morning of publication slapped with a libel lawsuit from Eaves For Women, the domestic violence charity whose hapless forays into research are touched on in this book.

If their work had been published in academic journals, anyone writing to correct their numbers would have been treated professionally. But this was not academia I was dealing with. Obviously, I did not write anything about Eaves that could not be verified, and just as obviously, they had not been sent a pre-publication copy of the book by my publisher but had been given one by book reviewer – and Eaves board member – Julie Bindel. The firm representing Eaves in this lawsuit threat? The one with Bindel's wife as a founding partner.

The Eaves claims would have been hilarious if they had not been so ludicrous. They claimed I "hacked their servers" to get information about their income and expenditures (as with all UK charities, it's public information available on government websites) and "broken confidentiality agreements" to discuss their research (I looked up their publications from conferences, also available online). Their arguments depended on evidence so far-fetched it could have served as a bad science example in the book itself.

I later learned this was not the first time this had happened. Eaves had threatened to sue so many people, so often, they even served legal threats on Bindel's own employer at the time, the Guardian newspaper for an article by Belinda Brooks-Gordon. (Bindel is no longer on Guardian staff.) The intellectual dishonesty of someone like Bindel, who claims to be 'silenced' and a 'free speech' advocate yet uses archaic laws to try to silence opposition, is staggering.

Unsurprisingly the threatened suit was without merit and quickly dropped.

Meanwhile, the media feminists of the UK ramped up the pressure. Julie Burchill wrote one article claiming I was a "sex addict," another calling me a "human toilet," and compared me to a convicted (and executed) Nazi war criminal. This was especially offensive as I am of Jewish heritage. The "feminist" literature magazine that published those last two tidbits claimed they did not know what the words meant. Sorry, *Mslexia*, but ignorance is no excuse. They did not apologize.

In Australia, feminist blogger Mia Freedman wrote weeks' worth of articles calling me disgusting, immoral, and worse because I had (apparently) not been friendly or chatty enough to her in the green room before we appeared for a debate on *Q&A*. Her wide network of mummy bloggers – and interns who work for millionaire Mia for free – spread the word that I was an easy target, sending an army of social media trolls my way. Including one disturbed young man posting from a Mammamia IP address about how my face should have been 'cut' after he came on it. One feminist turned up at a talk in Edinburgh to shout to the audience that I was a pedophile and claim screenshots of the Glasgow City Council's website (showing how much they paid for anti-strip club consultations) were faked. Others picketed talks and book signings, sent death threats, and harassed me so frequently by phone that I gave up on carrying a mobile altogether. They contacted my former editor at the *Telegraph* in an attempt to get me fired – weeks after I'd already left.

Few seem to care that the people doing this are all a couple of degrees of separation from known anti-LGBT and white supremacist orgs in the US. All anyone wants is to see the naughty, naughty sex lady be punished. They don't care how it's done or who does it.

This, I was told, was the price of being a sex worker in public.

Writers with the left-leaning New Statesman magazine, many of whom launched careers by harassing trans women and sex workers, also got the boot in. Such as Sarah Ditum, whose career was going nowhere until she changed from sex-positive features writer to "gender critical" thinker on "modern slavery." Kicking down pays! The magazine's assistant editor, Helen Lewis, sits on the board of a charity that is anti-sex work and anti-trans women. She and other feminists joked on social media when a former partner tried to sue me for reporting his abuse. (He later dropped the suit to much less fanfare.)

They encouraged Breitbart to run a week-long campaign of harassment and abuse. They egged on nasty "investigative journalist" Jeremy Duns who made sexual threats against me and my husband. They examined photos from my escorting days, speculating about what diseases I might have, or whether I was "hot enough" have been a sex worker (admission: my photos were terrible, I mean, pastel satin elbow gloves? Not that clients cared).

They circulated a list at public events suggesting that I and others were employed by a shadowy "Pimp Lobby" and financially benefitting from trafficking. If that's the case, I have yet to receive a paycheck. The laughable list, compiled by Julie Bindel, included a number of people uninvolved with sex work at all, including an artist who died in 2010. Fact-checking is not a valued quality among these people.

The abuse peaked when they bullied and outed a trans camgirl whose Twitter account they claimed had been written by me. It wasn't - but in the process they humiliated a woman who was not yet out to her family. Their supposed evidence? We both supported Scottish independence, and both, at different times, used the phrase "snake oil." In spite of having got it drastically wrong, there was no apology to the woman they doxxed.

Why would anyone do this? In short, to control the narrative. It would be unthinkable to have a discussion about women's rights that did not involve any women. Or a discussion about race that did not include people of color. But time and again when the topic is sex work, sex workers are not simply ignored, they are actively excluded.

What do sex workers want? A seat at the table. To be able to work together for safety. To report crimes against them without fear of arrest. For services to be made available that are not dependent on them giving evidence against others. To not live in fear of deportation or abuse by police. In short: they want the same protection under the law that any other worker can expect.

And not only is this what sex workers want, it's what the evidence supports as best practice. We've seen the benefits of decriminalization in New Zealand, in New South Wales Australia. We've also seen what goes wrong in Sweden, in the Netherlands, and in the US. International agencies from the WHO to Amnesty agree.

What happened to me was not the first nor even worst example. The very same second-wave feminists have harassed trans politicians out of their jobs, driven black cultural commentators off of social media, and consistently outed and trashed any sex worker who crosses their paths. Heaven help you if you happen to belong to more than one of these groups. They reserve the worst treatment for the most marginalized, secure in the knowledge that society does not care because they told society not to.

The disinformation campaign was a glimpse into a post-truth world where what matters is not what is right, but who can get the most money. Some of those folks were so threatened by a book that they tried to bankrupt, discredit, and silence one blogger. A movement backed by billions of dollars in grants is so susceptible to people seeing the real data, they will stop at nothing to keep the truth from getting out.

They are not interested in ethical debate. They demand that their point of view be bowed to, even (and especially) if that means keeping the discussion centered on their feelings rather than other people's right to exist in safety. They use the media not to promote understanding, but to bludgeon enemies. They do not care if their information is incorrect. I started off believing that open debate was the best way to win hearts and minds. I ended up realizing that some people will use that to drown out anyone who does not agree with their intolerant, hate-filled views. There is no way to have a debate with people who characterize you as an "orifice" who "should be dead in a ditch." There is no common ground to be found with people who willingly promote your abusers.

Instead of campaigning for migration justice, for racial equality to be upheld in law enforcement, for the end of austerity, against conditions that keep people in poverty, this is how they choose to use their platforms. Not in ending structural injustices that make sex work a profitable - sometimes the only profitable - choice, but in punishing the people who must make that choice.

The evidence-driven support for decrim hasn't come out of thin air. Much has been written on the disruptive effects of social media, but this much is true: if not for the internet, people like me would never have been able to challenge the stereotypes with facts. Marginalized people with multiple oppressions – black trans sex workers, drug using sex workers – who would otherwise fear being outed, are being taken seriously by a mainstream that otherwise would never have known they existed. The infantilized victims who need rich white ladies to save them, it turns out, are fully capable adults who can make their own decisions and won't hesitate to tell you that. And that makes some folks with vested interests very upset indeed.

And yet. In all the negativity, there are signs of light.

In the years from when I was a sex worker in 2003, since I came out in 2009, and after the first edition of this book in 2012, the ground has rapidly shifted. When Amnesty International rejected threats from famous feminists and backed the decriminalization of sex work based on the evidence, it was a win for a sex workers' movement that far predates and will long outlast any one person.

When I gave evidence to UK Parliament in 2016, the MPs – to my surprise – took the suggestions of sex workers on board in their report, rather that listening to entrenched and well-funded special interests. In Scottish Parliament, Rhoda Grant (who receives funding from the anti-gay, anti-abortion charity Care) has tried three times to introduce criminalization of sex work, and been defeated all three times. Evidence really does win out from time to time. It might not seem that way in the moment, but things are changing, slowly and surely.

The other side tried with legal threats and violence to silence people like me. It didn't work. We're not going anywhere.

In 2009 and 2012, it felt as if every week brought new abuse from a media obsessed with surfaces instead of content. So-called progressives shame and rejects sex workers who were early supporters of feminism, gay rights, and other movements that have since gained public acceptance on the back of that effort. In particular the most marginalized sex workers from black and trans communities were the ones most likely to be erased. People like Sylvia Rivera, Marsha P Johnson, and many more. Slowly and surely their legacy is being reclaimed, too.

The pendulum of attitudes about sex and sexuality is always in motion. I hope that in my lifetime the burden of shame felt by so many for so long will be lifted. With evidence and hard work we can reclaim the narrative and take back our lives from the playground bullies of shame and fear.

ACKNOWLEDGMENTS

This book would not have been possible without the work of many researchers to whom I am indebted. In particular work by Belinda Brooks-Gordon, Teela Sanders, and Laura Agustín has been especially enlightening.

I have been fortunate to get help on collecting data and finding information from loads of people. In particular I would like to thank Wendy Lyon, Jane Fae Ozimek, and Catherine Stephens. Alex Zhavoronkov is the creator of the useful Funding Trends website. Shout outs to Madison Young and Maxine Holloway for a place to crash and an excellent library to plunder. Special thanks to Furrygirl whose blogging on the diplomatic cables proved invaluable.

Thank you to Alex Feis-Bryce, who was enormously helpful when I appeared in front of Parliament, and Paris Lees, for being an incredible support and inspiration.

Thank you to the team who have supported me at every stage, from Patrick Walsh and Michael Burton, to my long-time editor Genevieve Pegg.

I would not have survived the last few years if not for the steadfast support of friends: Laura Lee, Matt Garner, Maggie McNeill, Paul Duane, Chris Nicholson, Steph Davy, and Nick Wilde.

Finally, I would like to thank my husband, who was the first reader of this work and a worthy foil in our debates on the topics involved.

ABOUT THE AUTHOR

Brooke Magnanti, one of Observer's "Faces of 2009" and Guardian newspaper's "Best British Weblog 2003," is a scientist and author. She is writer of the bestselling Belle de Jour series of books, which were adpated into the hit ITV show "Secret Diary of a Call Girl" starring Billie Piper. She is also the writer of The Sex Myth.

Brooke has been featured by more than 100 media outlets including the Sunday Times, Independent, New Scientist, Grazia, The Scotsman, HardTalk, Sky News, This Week and Newsnight. She is a columnist for the Telegraph's Wonder Women, former science editor of Cliterati, and has contributed pieces to the Guardian, Big Issue, and Town. Brooke was featured in an episode of Stephen Fry's Planet Word and is a popular public speaker on the themes of biometric and forensic science, sexualisation and popular culture, and internet anonymity and identity.

Brooke was born in west central Florida in 1975. She was a National Merit Scholar and received a B.Sc. from Florida State University in 1996, where she studied in the Anthropology and Mathematics departments. She later studied for a master's in Genetic Epidemiology at the University of Sheffield in England, and earned a Ph.D. in the Forensic Pathology department there, specialising in human decomposition and postmortem identification. She has worked in forensic science, epidemiology, chemoinformatics and cancer research. Brooke currently lives in the United States with her husband.

[i] 23 November 2010, available at:
http://www.theyworkforyou.com/debates/?id=2010-11-23c.235.0

[ii] Eleanor Mills, 'OMG: Porn in cyberspace,' *The Sunday Times*, 19 December 2010

[iii] ML Ybarra, KJ Mitchell, M Hamburger, M Diener-West, P Leaf, 'X-rated material and perpetration of sexually aggressive behavior among children and adolescents: is there a link?,' *Aggressive Behavior*, 2011, 37(1), 863–874

[iv] Summary articles, survey results, and additional material available at:
http://www.psychologies.co.uk/put-porn-in-its-place/

[v] Available at: http://www.socialcostsofpornography.org/

[vi] American Psychological Association, *Report of the APA Task Force on the Sexualization of Girls*, APA, Washington, DC, 2007

[vii] Australian Senate, 'Inquiry into the sexualization of children in the contemporary media environment,'
http://www.aph.gov.au/Senate/committee/eca_ctte/sexualization_of_children/tor.htm, 2007

[viii] http://www.slightlyrightofcentre.com/2011/10/industry-sources-isp-porn-filter-plans.html

[ix] NM Malamuth, T Addison, M Koss, 'Pornography and Sexual Aggression: Are there reliable effects and can we understand them?,' *Annual Review of Sex Research*, 2000, 11:26–91

[x] C Shipman, C Kazdin. 'Teens: Oral Sex and Casual Prostitution No Biggie,' ABCnews.go.com, 28 May 28 2009

[xi] Melissa Benn. 'Living Dolls, By Natasha Walter The Equality Illusion, By Kat Banyard,' The Independent, 05 March 2010

[xii] Wellings et al., 'Sexual behaviour in Britain: early heterosexual experience,' *The Lancet*, 2001, 358(9296): 1843–1850

[xiii] London School of Hygiene and Tropical Medicine, 'First global analysis

of sexual behaviour' press release, 30 October 2006

[xiv] Wellings, et al., 'Sexual behaviour in context: a global perspective,' *The Lancet*, 2006, 368(9548): 1706–1728

[xv] Centers for Disease Control, 'United States All Years: Percentage of Students Who Ever Had Sexual Intercourse' available at: http://apps.nccd.cdc.gov/yrbss/QuestYearTable.asp?path=byHT&ByVar =CI&cat=4&quest=Q58&year=Trend&loc=XX.

[xvi] Carmine Sarracino, Kevin Scott, Beacon Press, Boston, 2008

[xvii] R Nixon, 'Statement About the Report of the Commission on Obscenity and Pornography,' October 24, 1970, archived at: http://www.presidency.ucsb.edu/ws/index.php?pid=2759

[xviii] 'Corrections and clarifications,' *Guardian*. January 2009, http://www.guardian.co.uk/theguardian/2009/jan/12/corrections

[xix] T Hunt. 'Betting shops and strip clubs stand as monuments to New Labour morality' *The Guardian*, 2009, available at: <http://www.guardian.co.uk/commentisfree/2009/aug/06/labour-moral-market-gambling-society> Accessed 28 December 2010.

[xx] 'Sex assaults down since lap dance clubs opened' *Newquay Voice*, 3 March 2010, http://www.newquayvoice.co.uk/news/5/article/2950/

[xxi] P Bryant, D Linz, B Shafer, 'Government regulation of adult businesses through zoning and anti-nudity ordinances: Debunking the legal myth of negative secondary effects,' *Communication Law and Policy*, 2001, 6(2): pp 355–91

[xxii] JL Hanna, 'Exotic Dance Adult Entertainment: A Guide for Planners and Policy Makers' *Journal of Planning Literature, 2005,* 20(2), pp 116–134

[xxiii] G Dines, B Jensen, A Russo, *Pornography: The Production and Consumption of Inequality*, Routledge, Oxford, 1997

[xxiv] Beacon Press, 2010

[xxv] Jameson Berkow, 'Porn to get .xxx domain,' *Financial Post*, 25 June 2010

xxvi Tony Comstock. 'Is That a Boiled Frog in Your Pocket? Or Are You Just Happy to See Me?,' *The Atlantic*, 12 February 2011

xxvii Catharine A MacKinnon, 'Pornography as Defamation and Discrimination,' 71 B.U. L. Rev. 793 (1991)

xxviii Melinda Wenner Mover, 'The Sunny Side of Smut,' *Scientific American Mind*, 22 July 2011, p34

xxix Aleksandar Štulhofer, Vesna Buško and Ivan Landripet, 'Pornography, Sexual Socialization, and Satisfaction Among Young Men,' *Archives of Sexual Behavior*, February 2010, Volume 39, Number 1, 168–178

xxx Alan McKee, 'The relationship between attitudes towards women, consumption of pornography, and other demographic variables in a survey of 1023 consumers of pornography,' *International Journal of Sexual Health*, 2007, 19(1), pp31– 45

xxxi 'Are the effects of pornography negligible?' December 2009, http://www.eurekalert.org/pub_releases/2009-12/uom-ate120109.php 01

xxxii T D Kendall, 'Pornography, Rape, and the Internet' working manuscript, July 2007, available at: http://www.toddkendall.net/internetcrime.pdf

xxxiii Anthony D'Amato, 'Porn Up, Rape Down,' available at: *anthonydamato.law.northwestern.edu/Adobefiles/porn.pdf*

xxxiv G Dahl, S DellaVigna, 'Does Movie Violence Increase Violent Crime?,' *The Quarterly Journal of Economics*, 2009, 124:2, 677–734

xxxv R Green, *Sexual Science and the Law*, Harvard University Press, 1992

xxxvi Article 8, March 1998, http://www.sexed.org/archive/article08.html

xxxvii E Marriott 'Men and porn,' *Guardian Weekend*, 8 November 2003

xxxviii Rimm, *Georgetown Law Journal*, 1995, volume 83, June, pp1849–1934

xxxix 'How *Time* magazine promoted a Cyberhoax,' 19 July 1995, http://www.fair.org/media-beat/950719.html

[xl] Paula Petrik, 'Capitalists with rooms: Prostitution in Helena, Montana, 1865–. 1900,' *Montana: The Magazine of Western History* 31, Spring 1981, 33–45

[xli] GM Blackburn, SL Ricards, 'The prostitutes and gamblers of Virginia City, Nevada 1870,' *Pacific Historical Review*, 48, 1979, 239–58

[xlii] Thaddeus Russell, *A Renegade History of the United States*, Free Press/Simon & Schuster, 2010

[xliii] TJ Gilfoyle, *City of Eros: New York City, prostitution, and the commercialization of sex, 1790–1920*, WW Norton, 1994

[xliv]

http://webarchive.nationalarchives.gov.uk/+/http://www.homeoffice.gov.uk/crime-victims/reducing-crime/prostitution/

[xlv] L Agustin, 'Introduction to the Cultural Study of Commercial Sex,' *Sexualities*, 2007, 10; 403

[xlvi] C Benson, R Matthews, 'Street Prostitution: Ten Facts in Search of a Policy,' *International Journal of Sociology of the Law*, 1995, vol 23, pp395–415

[xlvii] Ronald Weitzer. 'New Directions in Research on

Prostitution,' *Crime, Law, and Social Change* 2005, 43, 211–35.

[xlviii] AL Daalder, *Lifting the Ban on Brothels: Prostitution in 2000–2001*, Netherlands Ministry of Justice, 2004

[xlix] John F. Decker, *Prostitution: Regulation and Control*, Publications of Criminal Law Education and Research Center, New York University, V. 13

[l] C Woodward et al, *Selling Sex in Queensland 2003: A study of prostitution in Queensland*, Prostitution Licensing Authority, *2004*

[li] *The Challenge of Change: A study of Canada's criminal prostitution laws*, Communication Canada, Ottawa, 2006

[lii] Roger Matthews, Home Office Police Research Group, 1993

[liii] T Sanders, 'The risks of street prostitution: punters, police, and

protesters,' *Urban Studies*, 2004, 41: 1703–1717

[liv] K Pease, 'Crime reduction 2003 in M Maguire, R Morgan, R Reiner (eds), The Oxford Handbook of Criminology, Oxford University Press, Oxford, 948–979

[lv] M Horne, 'Safety tips texted to prostitutes after tolerance zone ends,' *The Scotsman*, 8 June 2008

[lvi] K Keane, 18 November 2008, 'Prostitution "forced into city"', http://news.bbc.co.uk/1/hi/scotland/7734480.stm

[lvii] Conor Gallagher. "Dramatic rise in attacks on sex workers since law change" Irish Times, 4 September 2017

[lviii] http://www.conference-board.org/utilities/pressDetail.cfm?press_ID=3075

[lix] L Clark, 'Four in ten new teachers quit over red tape and unruly pupils,' *Daily Mail*, 10 July 2008

[lx] M Farley, A Cotton, J Lynne, S Zumbeck, F Spiwak, ME Reyes, D Alvarez, U Sezgin, 'Prostitution and trafficking in nine countries: An update on violence and posttraumatic stress disorder,' *Journal of Trauma Practice*, v 2 no 3 2003, p33–74

[lxi] B Brooks-Gordon, 'Memorandum of Evidence on the Criminal Justice and Immigration Bill,' British Psychological Society, 2008

[lxii] Full text of the complaint available at: http://deepthroated.files.wordpress.com/2011/09/complainttoapa_melissa farley.pdf

[lxiii] Pamela Stephenson, Julie Bindel, 'Prostitution: sex, lies and exploitation,' *Guardian*, 25 September 2009

[lxiv] 'Big Increase of Sex Workers a Myth: Latest Research,' Christchurch School of Medicine and Health Sciences, 2006-09-12

[lxv] 'Report of the Prostitution Law Review Committee on the Operation of the Prostitution Reform Act 2003' available at:

http://www.justice.govt.nz/policy-and-
consultation/legislation/prostitution-law-review-
committee/publications/plrc-report/report-of-the-prostitution-law-review-
committee-on-the-operation-of-the-prostitution-reform-act-2003

[lxvi] G Abel, L Fitzgerald, C Healy, (eds), 'Taking the crime out of sex work:
New Zealand sex workers' fight for decriminalization,' Policy Press, 2010

[lxvii] Laura Agustín, 'Big claims, little evidence: Sweden's law against buying
sex,' *The Local*, 23 July 2010, available at:
http://www.lauraagustin.com/ban-on-purchase-of-sex-helps-prevent-and-
combat-prostitution-says-swedish-evaluation

[lxviii] "Transsexual prostitutes in Paris face increasing violence" France 24, 08
September 2017

[lxix] Ari Brynjólfsson. "An enormous increase in prostitution in Iceland"
Pressan.ie, 28 June 2017.

[lxx] Mary Laing, Robert Comber. "Technologies and Social Justice Outcomes
in Sex Work Charities: Fighting Stigma, Saving Lives" *Proceedings of the 2017
CHI Conference on Human Factors in Computing Systems* Doi: 3025453.3025615

[lxxi] Bedford v. Canada ruling, full document available at:
www.cbc.ca/news/pdf/bedford-ruling.pdf

[lxxii] Kalyaan, 'Evidence to HAC, HC 23-II, Sixth Report on Human
Trafficking in the UK'

[lxxiii] Denis MacShane, 'Tackling the trafficking myths,' *Guardian*, 16
November 2009

[lxxiv] L Cusick, H Kinnell, B Brooks-Gordon, R Campbell, 'Wild Guesses
and Conflated Meanings: Estimating the size of the sex worker population
in Britain,' *Journal of Critical Social Policy*, 2009, Vol 29(4), pp703–719

[lxxv] H Kinnell, 'Sex workers in England and Wales: Briefing paper for
Department of Health, National Sexual Health Strategy' Europap-UK,
December 1999

[lxxvi] http://www2.ohchr.org/english/law/protocoltraffic.htm

[lxxvii] Julie Bindel. 'Penalizing the punters' *Guardian G2*, 21 November 2008, p16

[lxxviii] *Trafficking in Persons Report*, Office to Monitor and Combat Trafficking in Persons, US Department of State, 4 June 2008

[lxxix] 'Have sex traffic levels been exaggerated?,' *Newsnight*, 21 October 2009, available at: http://news.bbc.co.uk/1/hi/programmes/newsnight/8318629.stm

[lxxx] J Edwards, D Boffey, '25000 ex slaves on the streets of Britain' *Daily Mirror*, 19 October 2005

[lxxxi] Nick Davies, 'Prostitution and trafficking – the anatomy of a moral panic,' *The Guardian*, 20 October 2009

[lxxxii] Nick Davies, 'Inquiry fails to find single trafficker who forced anybody into prostitution,' *The Guardian*, 20 October 2009

[lxxxiii] 'United Kingdom Pentameter 2 statistics of victims recovered and suspects arrested during the operational phase,' United Kingdom Human Trafficking Centre, http://www.soca.gov.uk/about-soca/library/doc.../122-uk-pentameter-2-statistics

[lxxxiv] 'More or Less,' BBC Radio 4, 9 January 2009

[lxxxv] Tom Whitehead, 'Two in three rescued women have vanished again;, *The Daily Telegraph*, 16 September 2009

[lxxxvi] The Northern Ireland Department of Justice (DoJ), 'A Strategy to manage women offenders and those vulnerable to offending behaviour 2010–2013'

[lxxxvii] Available at http://www.publications.parliament.uk/pa/jt200506/jtselect/jtrights/245/24508.htm

[lxxxviii] BBC Radio 4, ibid

[lxxxix] Available at:

www.acpo.police.uk/.../Setting%20the%20Record%20(Project%20ACUM
EN)%20Aug%202010.pdf

[xc] R Edwards, 'Up to 12,000 foreign "sex slaves" work in British brothels'
Telegraph, 18 August 2010

[xci] Available at: www.soca.gov.uk/about-soca/library/doc_download/184-
nrm-annual-data-april-2009-to-march-2010

[xcii] *Wrong kind of victim? Full Report*, The Anti Trafficking Monitoring Group,
June 2010, available at:
http://www.antislavery.org/english/what_we_do/programme_and_advoca
cy_work/anti_trafficking_monitoring_group.aspx

[xciii] Catherine Bennett, 'No trafficking? Well, there's a hell of a lot of women
suffering,' *Observer on Sunday*, 25 October 2009

[xciv] Nikole Hannah-Jones, 'Analysis: Despite reputation, no proof Portland
is a hub for child sex trafficking,' *The Oregonian*, 13 January 2011

[xcv] RJ Estes and NA Weiner. *The Commercial Sexual Exploitation of Children In
the US, Canada and Mexico*, University of Pennsylvania School of Social
Work Center for the Study of Youth Policy, 19 September 2001

[xcvi] Elizabeth Nolan Brown. "Human-Trafficking Arrests Are Very Rare in
Most States" *Reason*, 25 September 2017.

[xcvii] Norma Jean Almodovar. "Operation Do The Math."
http://www.policeprostitutionandpolitics.com

[xcviii] Lara Powers. "Why a mom's Facebook warning about human
traffickers hurts sex-trafficked kids" Los Angeles Times, April 3rd, 2017

[xcix] Elizabeth Nolan Brown. "Child Sex-Trafficking Victim Sentenced to
Nearly Six Years in Prison for Child Sex-Trafficking" *Reason*, 30 August
2017.

[c] US Bureau of Justice, *Human Trafficking/Trafficking in Persons*,
http://bjs.ojp.usdoj.gov/index.cfm?ty=tp&tid=40

[ci] Bureau of Justice Statistics, Office of Justice Programs, US Department of

Justice Press Release, 15 January 2009

cii Elizabeth Nolan Brown, "American Sex Police," Reason, 14 March 2017

ciii Deborah Gibbs, Jennifer Hardison, et al. Evaluation of Services for Domestic Minor Victims of Human Trafficking National Criminal Justice Reference Service NCJ 248578, August 2014.

civ The Lancet, Editorial. "Keeping sex workers safe: Volume 386, No. 9993, p504, 8 August 2015

cv A transcript from the Courts Service Courts Accounts System showing "poor box" payments made to Ruhama from 2007 to March 2016. Obtained by UglyMugs.ie under FOI on 30 September 2016. Accessed at: https://uglymugs.ie/2016/09/30/foi-courts-service-re-ruhama/

cvi Anne Elizabeth Moore. "Special Report: Money and Lies in Anti-Human Trafficking NGOs" January 27, 2015, Truth-out.org

cvii Anne Elizabeth Moore. "The American Rescue Industry: Toward an Anti-Trafficking Paramilitary" April 08, 2015, Truth-out.org

cviii Pamela Engle. "Senator asks for more scrutiny of human trafficking grants" Scripps Howard wire service, September 16, 2011.

cix Marjie Lunstrom and Sam Stanton. "Donors slip away from sex trafficking nonprofit" Sacramento Bee, 08 May 2017

cx Elizabeth Nolan Brown. "Courage House Claimed to Save Sex-Trafficked Girls. Instead, It Used Them As Funding Bait While Playing Evangelical Christian Missionary" Reason, 20 September 2016

cxi D Harwell. "Workers endured long hours, low pay at Chinese factory used by Ivanka Trump's clothing-maker" Washington Post, 25 April 2017.

cxii K Shannon, S Strathdee, et al. "Structural and Environmental Barriers to Condom Use Negotiation With Clients Among Female Sex Workers: Implications for HIV-Prevention Strategies and Policy" American Journal of Public Health April 2009 cxiii K Shannon, M Rusch et al. "Mapping violence and policing as an environmental–structural barrier to health service and syringe availability among substance-using women in street-level sex work" *International Journal of Drug Policy* Volume 19, Issue 2, April 2008, Pages 140-147

cxiv K Shannon, T Kerr et al. "Prevalence and structural correlates of gender based violence among a prospective cohort of female sex workers" *BMJ* 2009; 339 doi: https://doi.org/10.1136/bmj.b2939

cxv Diane Taylor and Mark Townsend "Mariana Popa was killed working as a prostitute. Are the police to blame?" *Guardian*, 19 Jan 2014.

cxvi Connelly, L, Jarvis-King, L and Ahearne, G. (2015) (eds.) 'Blurred Lines: The Contested Nature of Sex Work in a Changing Social Landscape' Special Edition of *The Graduate Journal of Social Science*, 11(3)

cxvii Jay Levy. *Criminalising the Purchase of Sex: Lessons from Sweden*. Routledge, 2014

cxviii S Dickson, *Sex in the City*, Eaves, 2004, available at: http://charlottegore.s3.amazonaws.com/media/DicksonSexinCotyPoppy07.pdf

cxix S Shuster, 'Prostitution: Ukraine's unstoppable export,' *Time*, 9 October 2010

cxx http://www.cablegatesearch.net/cable.php?id=06YEREVAN1019

cxxi Tara Conlan, Carmiola Ionescu, 'Monica's story: rescued victim of child traffickers or kidnapped by ITN crew?' *The Guardian*, 23 February 2008

cxxii Emily Jordan. "The Wrong Light": Sex, lies and the story of Mickey Choothesa. July 22, 2017. Salon.com

cxxiii Carola Häggkvist "Hannah, 22, pressades ljuga om att hon varit sexslav" Aftonbladet, 30 August 2017.

cxxiv Maud Effting, Anneke Stoffelen "Vrouw met een verleden" De

Volkskrant, 9 March 2013.

[cxxv] 'Caught Between the Tiger and the Crocodile,' available at: http://blip.tv/file/1159149

[cxxvi] Christopher Shay, Mom Kunthear, 'Study Slams Trafficking Law,' *The Phnom Penh Post*, 23 July 2009

[cxxvii] Robert Carmichael, 'Cambodia cracks down on the sex industry,' Deutsche Welle, 5 April 2010

[cxxviii] 'Off the Streets: Arbitrary Detention and Other Abuses against Sex Workers in Cambodia,' Human Rights Watch, July 2010

[cxxix] Maher, Page, et al. 'Conflicting Rights: How the Prohibition of Human Trafficking and Sexual Exploitation Infringes the Right to Health of Female Sex Workers in Phnom Penh, Cambodia.' *Health and Human Rights*. 2015 Jun 11;17(1):E102-13.

[cxxx] http://www.cablegatesearch.net/cable.php?id=06PHNOMPENH1607

[cxxxi] Julie Bindel, 'The Price of a Holiday Fling,' *Guardian*, 5 July 2003

[cxxxii] Grace Hammond. 'Why money has stripped away class barriers in the sex industry,' *Yorkshire Post*, 20 September 2010

[cxxxiii] Roz Kaveney. "Julie Burchill has ended up bullying the trans community" *Guardian*, 13 January 2013

Made in the USA
Lexington, KY
28 February 2018